WHEN MATT MURDOCK WAS A KID, HE LOST HIS SIGHT IN AN ACCIDENT INVOLVING A TRUCK CARRYING RADIOACTIVE CHEMICALS. THOUGH HE COULD NO LONGER SEE, THE CHEMICALS HEIGHTENED MURDOCK'S OTHER SENSES AND IMBUED HIM WITH AN AMAZING 360-RADAR SENSE. NOW MATT USES HIS ABILITIES TO FIGHT FOR HIS CITY. HE IS THE ***MAN WITHOUT FEAR.*** HE IS...*DAREDEVIL!*

BEGINNING ANEW AFTER THE WORLD FORGOT DAREDEVIL'S IDENTITY, MATT CAME BACK TO NEW YORK AND STARTED PRACTICING LAW AGAIN. MATT'S RETURN WAS HERALDED BY A MAJOR VICTORY AS HE SUCCESSFULLY ARGUED A CASE IN THE SUPREME COURT, LEGITIMIZING SUPER HEROES' ROLE IN THE LEGAL SYSTEM. ONE OF MATT'S GREATEST ENEMIES, WILSON FISK, A.K.A. THE KINGPIN, HAD BEEN SECRETLY UNDERWRITING MATT'S OPPOSITION. FACED WITH A RARE DEFEAT, FISK HAS VOWED TO USE HIS VAST RESOURCES TO MAINTAIN HIS GRIP ON THE CITY...

CHARLES SOULE
WRITER

STEFANO LANDINI (*Nos. 595-597*) & RON GARNEY (*Nos. 598-600*)
ARTISTS

MATT MILLA
COLOR ARTIST

"THEY ALSO SERVE" FROM *DAREDEVIL No. 600*

CHRISTOS GAGE WRITER
MIKE PERKINS ARTIST
ANDY TROY COLOR ARTIST

VC's CLAYTON COWLES
LETTERER

BILL SIENKIEWICZ (*Nos. 595*) AND DAN MORA & JUAN FERNANDEZ (*Nos. 596-600*)
COVER ART

ANNALISE BISSA & CHRISTINA HARRINGTON ASSISTANT EDITORS
MARK BASSO ASSOCIATE EDITOR
JORDAN WHITE WITH MARK PANICCIA EDITORS

COLLECTION EDITOR **MARK D. BEAZLEY**
ASSISTANT EDITOR **CAITLIN O'CONNELL**
ASSOCIATE MANAGING EDITOR **KATERI WOODY**
SENIOR EDITOR, SPECIAL PROJECTS **JENNIFER GRÜNWALD**
VP PRODUCTION & SPECIAL PROJECTS **JEFF YOUNGQUIST**
SVP PRINT, SALES & MARKETING **DAVID GABRIEL**
BOOK DESIGNER **ADAM DEL RE**
EDITOR IN CHIEF **C.B CEBULSKI**
CHIEF CREATIVE OFFICER **JOE QUESADA**
PRESIDENT **DAN BUCKLEY**
EXECUTIVE PRODUCER **ALAN FINE**

DAREDEVIL: BACK IN BLACK VOL. 6 — MAYOR FISK. Contains material originally published in magazine form as DAREDEVIL #595-600. First printing 2018. ISBN 978-1-302-91062-4. Published by MARVEL WORLDWIDE, INC., a subsidiary of MARVEL ENTERTAINMENT, LLC. OFFICE OF PUBLICATION: 135 West 50th Street, New York, NY 10020. **Printed in Canada.** DAN BUCKLEY, President, Marvel Entertainment; JOHN NEE, Publisher; JOE QUESADA, Chief Creative Officer; TOM BREVOORT, SVP of Publishing; DAVID BOGART, SVP of Business Affairs & Operations, Publishing & Partnership; DAVID GABRIEL, SVP of Sales & Marketing, Publishing; JEFF YOUNGQUIST, VP of Production & Special Projects; DAN CARR, Executive Director of Publishing Technology; ALEX MORALES, Director of Publishing Operations; DAN EDINGTON, Managing Editor; SUSAN CRESPI, Production Manager; STAN LEE, Chairman Emeritus. For information regarding advertising in Marvel Comics or on Marvel.com, please contact Vit DeBellis, Custom Solutions & Integrated Advertising Manager, at vdebellis@marvel.com. For Marvel subscription inquiries, please call 888-511-5480. **Manufactured between 6/1/2018 and 7/3/2018 by SOLISCO PRINTERS, SCOTT, QC, CANADA.**

10 9 8 7 6 5 4 3 2 1

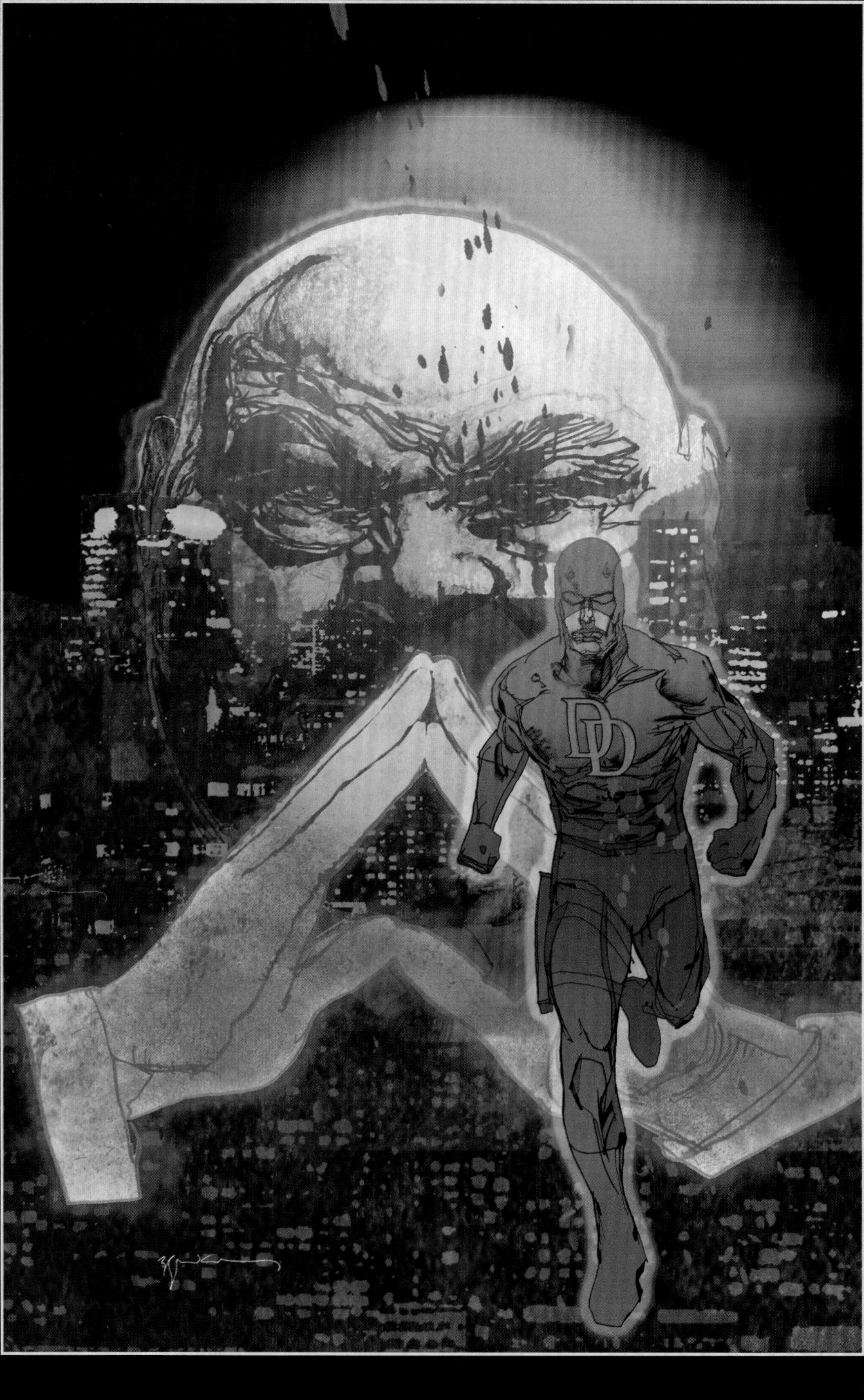

595

A BOY WAS BORN IN NEW YORK CITY.
AS HE GREW, HE CAME TO SEE THAT THE CITY HE LOVED WAS A PLACE OF DARKNESS AND VIOLENCE--FAR FROM WHAT IT COULD BE.
BUT THIS BOY HAD VISION.
ANOTHER NEW YORK EXISTED--A SHINING BEACON, WITH EVERYTHING AND EVERYONE IN ITS PLACE. HE COULD SEE IT.
THINGS COULD CHANGE.
HE COULD CHANGE THEM.
AND HE WOULD.
THIS WORK COST THE BOY THE LOVE OF HIS LIFE.
FOR A TIME, IT EVEN COST HIM HIS SIGHT.
BUT NEVER HIS VISION.
HE NEVER STOPPED--NO MATTER THE OBSTACLES IN HIS WAY. HE COULD NOT STOP.
WILSON FISK KNEW HOW TO FIX THE CITY, IF ONLY THEY WOULD LET HIM.
AND ONE DAY...

TIMES SQUARE.
NOW.
...THEY DID.
FISK
FISK NYC
FISK for NYC
HOW, FOGGY?

THE OTHER CANDIDATES WERE BUSINESS AS USUAL. FISK FELT DIFFERENT.
HE RAN AS AN INDEPENDENT, NO PARTY AFFILIATIONS, WASN'T IN ANYONE'S POCKET.
HE SAID HE WAS NEW YORK. HE'D LIVED IT POOR, HE'D LIVED IT RICH, HE KNEW IT UPTOWN AND DOWN. SAID HE KNEW WHAT WE NEEDED.

BUT DIDN'T PEOPLE FIGHT? HE'S A CRIME LORD.
OH, SURE. PLENTY OF OP-EDS, PLENTY OF PROTESTS, PLENTY OF EXPOSÉS.
FISK NEVER DENIED IT. NEVER EVEN ADDRESSED IT. JUST STAYED ON MESSAGE.
SAID PEOPLE KNEW WHAT HE WAS, AND WHAT HE WASN'T, AND WHAT HE COULD GIVE THEM.

HE TURNED EVERYONE'S PRE-CONCEPTIONS INTO A SELLING POINT. THAT BOOK HE PUT OUT HELPED, TOO.
HE MADE IT A NEW YORK THING--LIKE LIVING IN THIS CITY IS ALL ABOUT WORKING THE SYSTEM, KNOWING HOW TO GET THINGS DONE. BENDING THE RULES WHEN YOU NEED TO.
WHO BETTER TO DO THAT THAN THE KINGPIN OF CRIME?

FISK
FOR
NYC
HOW THE HELL DID THE KINGPIN BECOME THE MAYOR OF NEW YORK CITY?
IT WAS LIKE A DRIVE-BY SHOOTING, MATT.
FISK WAITED UNTIL THE LAST POSSIBLE DAY UNDER THE BOARD OF ELECTIONS' RULES TO ANNOUNCE HIS CANDIDACY.
IT WAS ALL SO *FAST.* MAYBE IF PEOPLE HAD MORE TIME TO *THINK,* BUT...THEY DIDN'T.

"AND THEN HE JUST...WON.
"I TRIED TO CALL YOU. TRIED TO TELL YOU WHAT WAS HAPPENING. BUT... YOU WERE GONE. OFF IN CHINA."
I JUST NEVER THOUGHT... I CAN'T BELIEVE THIS.
NO. THIS IS WRONG.
HE *CHEATED* SOMEHOW.
THERE IS *NO* WAY THEY PICKED HIM. I KNOW IT.
MATT... WHAT ARE YOU GOING TO DO?
COME ON, FOGGY. YOU ALREADY KNOW.

NEW YORK COUNTY DISTRICT ATTORNEY'S OFFICE.
"I'M GOING TO FIGHT."
I'VE KNOWN WILSON FISK FOR YEARS, MR. HOCHBERG.
I'M CONFIDENT WE CAN BUILD A CASE AGAINST HIM. ELECTION FRAUD SEEMS LIKE A GOOD BET.
AND IF NOT THAT, BELIEVE ME, I KNOW WHERE TO LOOK FOR DIRT ON HIM. WE'LL FIND SOMETHING. I'LL GET STARTED RIGHT AWAY--
YOU'RE A CRUSADER, MR. MURDOCK, AND YOUR ZEAL AND SKILL HAVE SERVED YOU WELL DURING YOUR TIME HERE. YOU'RE AN ASSET TO THIS OFFICE.
BUT THIS OFFICE IS STILL PART OF THE GREAT CITY OF NEW YORK.
WHAT ARE YOU SAYING, SIR?
I'M SAYING WE DO NOT GET TO SELECTIVELY IGNORE THE DIRECTIVES OF THE MAYOR.
AS IT STANDS, I CANNOT AUTHORIZE OPENING AN INVESTIGATION AGAINST WILSON FISK SIMPLY BECAUSE OF HIS REPUTATION.

ON A PERSONAL LEVEL, I HAVE NO DOUBT THAT FISK IS...OR WAS...A MONSTER, RESPONSIBLE FOR AWFUL THINGS LARGE AND SMALL.
BUT AS HE HIMSELF NOTED DURING HIS CAMPAIGN, VERY LITTLE OF THAT WAS EVER ACTUALLY PROVEN.
AND HE IS THE MAYOR THE CITY ELECTED.

SURVIVED THEM ALL.
JUST KEEP YOUR HEAD DOWN AND DO YOUR JOB WELL. FIND JUSTICE WHERE YOU CAN.
SPEAKING OF WHICH, I HAVE A NEW ASSIGNMENT FOR YOU.
I'M SORRY TO SAY THIS, BUT YOU WILL ABSOLUTELY HATE IT.

OUR NEWLY ELECTED MAYOR HAS ASKED US TO BUILD CASES GAINST THE VIGILANTES. IT WAS ONE OF HIS PRIMARY CAMPAIGN PROMISES, AND HE'S FOLLOWING THROUGH.
A CLAMPDOWN ON NON-GOVERNMENTAL EXERCISE OF AUTHORITY. SPIDER-MAN, LUKE CAGE, IRON FIST, MS. MARVEL, THE PUNISHER, ALL OF THEM.
DAREDEVIL.
AFRAID SO.

THE SUPREME COURT JUST ACKNOWLEDGED THE LEGITIMACY OF SUPER HEROES IN THE LEGAL FRAMEWORK, AND NOW WE'RE SUPPOSED TO TREAT THEM LIKE CRIMINALS?
FISK JUST WANTS THEM GONE SO THEY CAN'T TAKE HIM DOWN. I'M NOT DOING IT.
I KNOW ABOUT YOUR ASSOCIATION WITH THE... COSTUMED COMMUNITY, AND DAREDEVIL IN PARTICULAR.
I'M SURE IT'S A BLOW, MATT, BUT MY HANDS ARE TIED. YOUR NAME WAS MENTIONED SPECIFICALLY IN THE MAYOR'S REQUEST.

THE PEOPLE YOU NAMED... OTHER THAN THE PUNISHER, THOSE PEOPLE AREN'T VIGILANTES, SIR.
THEY'RE HEROES.

SON, I'M SORRY. BUT IN THIS CITY, RIGHT NOW...
...THEY'RE THE BAD GUYS.

LATER.
OKAY, WE CAN FIGHT THIS.
THE HAWK SAYS I HAVE TO INVESTIGATE DAREDEV FINE--BUT IT CAN TA A LONG TIME TO BUI A CASE. YOU KNOW THAT, ELLEN.
YEARS, SOMETIMES
YEAH, IT WASN'T MUCH, BUT IT WAS PAID OFF. HAVING A CAR IN THIS CITY IS A LUXURY, ESPECIALLY ON A PARALEGAL'S SALARY.
NICE TO BE ABLE TO GET OUT OF TOWN. SHARON AND I HAD SOME OF OUR FIRST DATES IN THAT CAR, DRIVING AROUND IN THE MOUNTAINS UPSTATE.
IF THE POLICE HAD DONE IT, I COULD'VE MADE A CLAIM AGAINST THE CITY. BUT WHAT AM I GONNA DO, SUE SPIDER-MAN?
THE DEDUCTIBLES ARE ***NUTS*** ON POWERS-RELATED INSURANCE, TOO. SO...THAT WAS THAT. IT'S THE BUS FOR ME NOW, OR THE SUBWAY.
NO MORE MOUNTAINS FOR THIS GIRL.
I'M SORRY. I KNOW YOU LOVE THE HEROES, BUT LIFE IN THIS CITY'S TOUGH ENOUGH AS IT IS.
SOMETIMES YOU JUST WANT A LITTLE NORMAL, YOU KNOW?
DID YOU VOTE FOR HIM, ELLEN?

SURE.

AND IN THE MEANTIME, WE CAN DIG INTO EVERY LAST VOTE CAST IN THIS ELECTION, EVERY CAMPAIGN CONTRIBUTION, EVERY DOLLAR FISK SPENT.
WHATEVER HE DID TO CHEAT HIS WAY INTO THE MAYOR'S OFFICE, WE WILL *FIND* IT. WORKING IN THE D.A.'S OFFICE GIVES US ACCESS TO ALL SORTS OF RECORDS, AND--

I EVER TELL YOU I USED TO HAVE A CAR, MATT?
UH... NO. YOU NEVER DID.

AND THEN SPIDER-MAN THREW IT AT THE RHINO.

MATT, I ADORE YOU, AND I LOVE WORKING FOR YOU...

...BUT THAT IS NONE OF YOUR BUSINESS.

Should I *quit?*
I successfully argued before the *Supreme Court.* Any firm in town would kill to have me on their masthead.
Or maybe I could put out a shingle with Foggy--if he'd have me. Hard to say. It's better between us, but it's not perfect.
Fisk *wants* me out of the D.A.'s office. It's obvious--that's why he told Hochberg to put me on the Daredevil investigation.
He doesn't know Matt Murdock is Daredevil, but he knows we're *connected.*
If I *quit,* I'm giving Fisk what he wants--but if I stay, I'll have to build a case against *myself.*
Credit where credit's due--it's a genius play.
Bah. I don't know. I'll have to--
HELP!
Yeah.

This is what I need.
What did the Hawk say?
Find justice where I can.

PFSSH
I'm *Daredevil.*
I *make* justice.

I *will* save my city from Wilson Fisk.

Even if I have to do it one night at a time.
KRCK
NNGH!
THWM
HELL'S KITCHEN IS MINE. I THOUGHT EVERY SCUMBAG IN THE CITY KNEW THAT.
I'M NOT A SCUMBAG.
COULD'VE FOOLED M--
Hm.

NOPE.
SPNG

KZZCK
AAAGH!
I HAVE A QUESTION.

WHAT KIND OF MUGGER CARRIES A *TASER?*

THIS KIND.

NYPD.
DAREDEVIL, YOU ARE UNDER ARREST. DROP THE BATON AND GET DOWN ON THE GROUND.
SLOWLY.
Damn.
DETECTIVE
1690

YOU, TOO?
YEAH, ME, TOO.
WE HAVE THE SUSPECT. ONE OFFICER DOWN, TASER. WE NEED MEDICAL HERE RIGHT AWAY.
How did I miss this?

Too distracted. Too focused on *Fisk.*
I MEAN IT. LOSE THE WEAPON, DOWN ON THE GROUND. I WON'T SAY IT AGAIN.
AND BEFORE YOU GET ANY IDEAS ABOUT TRYING TO FLY ON OUT OF HERE OR WHATEVER YOU DO, KNOW THAT WE'VE GOT OFFICERS ON THE ROOFTOPS.
EVEN IF YOU GET PAST US, THEY'VE GOT YOU DEAD TO RIGHTS.

So they do.
THIS IS ENTRAPMENT. IT'LL NEVER STICK.

YOUR BUDDY IN THE D.A.'S OFFICE BEEN TELLING YOU A FEW THINGS, *HUH?*
YOU KNOW WHAT HE'D TELL YOU IF HE WERE HERE RIGHT NOW? ONE WORD.
COMPLY.
I thought I'd have more time. Time to plan. Time to *fight.*

I should have known better.
KLNK

This is the Kingpin.

UPTOWN.
THANK YOU FOR SEEIN' ME, FISK. KNOW YOU GOTTA BE PRETTY BUSY THESE DAYS, WITH ALL THIS MAYOR STUFF GOIN' ON.
GUESS YOU'LL BE TAKING MEETINGS IN CITY HALL SOON. WHO'D EVER HAVE THOUGHT? LOVE IT.
Fisk knows a lot about Daredevil. More than almost anyone else-- including about my powers.
He knows I can hear this.
I JUST WANNA SAY, LORD KNOWS MY GUYS AND YOUR GUYS HAVE HAD OUR DIFFERENCES OVER THE YEARS, BUT THINGS BEEN GOOD FOR A WHILE BETWEEN US.
EVERYBODY DOIN' WELL, EVERYBODY MAKIN' MONEY.
WE THINK NOW...WELL, WITH YOU, UH, WORKING THE SYSTEM...IT'S PROBABLY GONNA GET EVEN BETTER.
WE KNOW THIS WAS YOUR PLAY, AND WE'LL RESPECT THAT. HOWEVER YOU WANT TO RUN THINGS IS GOOD BY US.
WE JUST WANT A PIECE. A SEAT ON THE GRAVY TRAIN.
AND SPEAKIN' ON BEHALF OF OUR SHARED FRATERNITY... LET ME SAY...
...WILSON, WE'RE PROUD OF YA.
The Mayor of New York is meeting with Hammerhead, one of the city's most notorious Maggia bosses. Talking business. Making plans.
WE WERE WORRIED AFTER MURDOCK PULLED THAT WHOLE SUPREME COURT THING, BUT YOU JUST SHOVED IT RIGHT BACK IN HIS FACE.
THING OF BEAUTY.
SO, ANYWAY, WHENEVER YOU WANNA PICK THINGS UP WITH US, LET US KNOW. USUAL CHANNELS.
And Fisk wants me to hear every single word.
NO. YOU AREN'T HERE FOR THAT.
That's him. No one else sounds like the Kingpin. Every word is a body blow. Like a fist hitting a side of beef.
YOU ARE HERE BECAUSE I WANT YOU TO KNOW ONE THING.
I WON. EVERYONE ELSE LOST.
NOW LEAVE. AND USE THE SIDE DOOR.
I HAVE A REPUTATION TO MAINTAIN.

HNH.
WHAT THE--
HEH.
MAYOR FISK. THING OF BEAUTY.
HE'LL SEE YOU NOW.

GOOD EVENING.
THANK YOU, OFFICERS. LEAVE HIM WITH ME.
YOUR HONOR, ARE YOU SURE? THIS IS DAREDEVIL... WE'RE NOT ENTIRELY SURE WHAT HE'S CAPABLE OF, AND--
LEAVE.
HIM.
UH, SURE, MR. MAYOR.
OF COURSE.
WE'LL BE RIGHT OUTSIDE IF YOU NEED US.
THEY'RE BOTH GOOD COPS, IF YOU'RE WONDERING. TRIED AND TRUE NYPD BLUE.
I ASKED FOR YOU, AND THEY BROUGHT YOU TO ME.
IT WAS THE EASIEST THING I'VE EVER DONE.

YOU WON'T GET AWAY WITH THIS, FISK.
GET AWAY WITH *WHAT?*
I WON AN ELECTION.

DO YOU THINK THE PEOPLE OF NEW YORK ENJOY YOU AND YOUR MASKED FRIENDS INVADING THEIR LIVES, DESTROYING THEIR PROPERTY, BRINGING CHAOS AND TERROR?
I DON'T.
THEY WANT IT TO STOP, AND I PROMISED THEM I'D STOP IT. THAT'S ALL.
TAP
WE BOTH LOVE THIS CITY, DAREDEVIL. WE SEE IT DIFFERENTLY--WHAT IT SHOULD BE--BUT WE BOTH LOVE IT.
WE HAVE THAT IN COMMON.
TAP
KCHK
BUT ONLY ONE OF US WAS ASKED TO SAVE IT.

NOT YOU. NEVER YOU.
ME.
ME.
I WANT YOU TO REMEMBER THAT, IN THE COMING DAYS. YOU APPOINTED YOURSELF THEIR SAVIOR, BUT THEY ACTUALLY CHOSE ME.
I WAS ABSOLUTELY CLEAR ABOUT WHAT I WOULD GIVE THEM. ORDER. NORMALCY. ACCOUNTABILITY. THINGS YOU AND YOUR KIND DON'T UNDERSTAND.
THEY KNOW WHAT I'M GOING TO DO, AND THEY ASKED ME TO DO IT.
TAP
KCLK
I DIDN'T.

WHAT NOW, HERO?
I'M THE MAYOR OF NEW YORK CITY.
NOT FOR LONG.
PFSSH
SMSH

SIR! ARE YOU ALL RIGHT? WHAT HAPPENED?
DAREDEVIL.
HE ATTACKED ME.
WHAT ARE YOU WAITING FOR, DETECTIVE?
GO GET HIM.

NYPD
DAN MORA

MANHATTAN.
MIDTOWN NORTH PRECINCT HOUSE.
WE'RE CALLING A LEVEL 4, INSPECTOR.

A LEVEL 4? WE HAVEN'T CALLED A LEVEL 4 SINCE 9/11, COMMISSIONER.
WHAT'S HAPPENING?
THE MAYOR WAS ASSAULTED UP IN HIS TOWER. SUSPECT FLED. WE NEED EVERYONE ON THIS. EVERY PRECINCT, ALL BOROUGHS, CITY-WIDE.
WE'RE SENDING THE DATA THROUGH THE SYSTEM NOW--YOUR DISPATCH SHOULD HAVE IT IN A MINUTE.
AND, INSPECTOR, SUSPECT IS A CODE PX.
PX. POWERS? A SUPER VILLAIN? MY GOD. ALL RIGHT, WE'LL MAKE SURE THE SPECIAL RESPONSE TEAMS ARE ACTIVATED.

CAN I ASK WHICH ONE, SIR?
IF IT'S THE SHOCKER, IT'S ONE THING, BUT IF IT'S, LIKE, BULLSEYE, THAT'S A TOTALLY DIFFERENT STORY.
NO. IT'S--

CODE PX ALERT. ALL UNITS ARE ADVISED TO BE ON THE LOOKOUT FOR METAHUMAN DAREDEVIL.
NYPD
CODE PX - Suspect: Daredevil
CIVILIAN IDENTITY: UNKNOWN
SUSPECT IS KNOWN TO BE AN EXTREMELY SKILLED HAND-TO-HAND COMBATANT WITH HEIGHTENED SENSES.
OTHER ABILITIES UNKNOWN. APPROACH WITH CAUTION.
ALIASES: MAN WITHOUT FEAR, HORNHEAD, DEVIL OF
A LEVEL 4. WOW. WHOLE DAMN DEPARTMENT AFTER ONE GUY.
NOT ANYMORE, I GUESS.
AND IT'S *DAREDEVIL*. I THOUGHT HE WAS... ISN'T HE A *GOOD* ONE?

DAREDEVIL? YOU EVER SEEN HIM FIGHT?
NAH. YOU?
YEAH. UNFORTUNATELY.
UNFORTUNATELY? WHAT THE HELL DOES THAT MEAN?
YOU KNOW HOW WE ALL TALK ABOUT HOW WE'D TAKE ONE OF THESE GUYS DOWN IF WE HAD TO? BLAST THE HUMAN TORCH WITH A FIRE EXTINGUISHER OR WHATEVER?
YEAH, SURE. OF COURSE.
DAREDEVIL ALWAYS SEEMED LIKE HE'D BE EASY. SORTA SEEMED LIKE JUST A GUY. NO EYE-BLASTS OR ANYTHING.
...
THEN I SAW HIM FIGHT.
SO WHAT DO YOU THINK? WE SHOULD CALL THE AVENGERS? LET THEM GET HIM?
HELL NO. THIS GUY ATTACKED THE MAYOR OF NEW YORK CITY. I DON'T CARE IF HE IS DAREDEVIL AND I DON'T CARE IF THE MAYOR'S THAT DIRTBAG FISK.
HE ATTACKED THE MAYOR, WHICH MEANS HE ATTACKED THE CITY, WHICH MEANS HE ATTACKED US. THIS IS OURS. PERIOD.
IT'S A MATTER OF PRIDE.

All right. Get past the anger. Get past the denial.
This is actually happening.
Kingpin is the mayor of New York City.
What does that even mean?
Think it through.
This isn't any different than when Stilt-Man shows up and goes "You're doomed, Daredevil, I've redesigned my legs and now they go twice as high!"
Fisk just found a way to upgrade his powers.

Fisk has City Hall. Okay. Fine.
He doesn't have the *city.*

Plenty of good people in New York. They know the score.
I can use that. Just need a *strategy.* Have to figure out how to *fight* him.
Just need a little time to *think.*

EEEOOO
EEEOOO

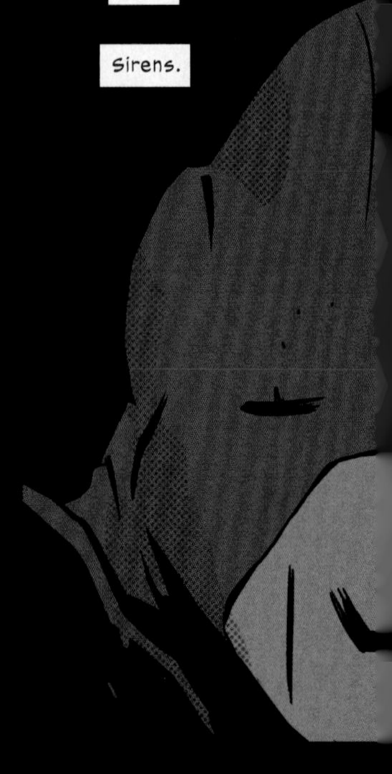
Wait.
Sirens.

That's a *big* deployment. I can hear helicopters, too. Getting close. They'll probably zip right overhead.
Must be serious. I should follow them--see if I can help.

WHF
WHF
WHF
WHF
Remind this city what a *hero* looks l--

DAREDEVIL! THIS IS THE NYPD! YOU ARE UNDER ARREST!
DROP THE WEAPON AND PUT YOUR HANDS BEHIND YOUR HEAD!
NYPD
WE'VE GOT POSITIVE I.D. ON THE SUSPECT, ON THE ROOF AT 691 8th AVENUE.
ROGER THAT. WE'VE GOT UNITS HEADED UP RIGHT NOW-- IN THE ELEVATORS. SHOULD HAVE HIM IN CUSTODY IN A MINUTE OR TWO.
UH, YOU MIGHT WANT TO HURRY THAT UP A LITTLE BIT. I THINK HE MIGHT--

DAMMIT! HE'S RUNNING! DOVE RIGHT OFF THE BUILDING!
DON'T LOSE SIGHT OF HIM! WE'RE SENDING MORE AIR SUPPORT TO YOUR LOCATION, INCLUDING A PX-EQUIPPED UNIT.
STAY ON HIM, FOR GOD'S SAKE!
PFSH
ACKNOWLEDGED. WE GOT THIS GUY.

Stupid, Matt, so stupid.
This is what Fisk wanted all along. Why he had me brought in. Why he let me keep my mask on.
He got me mad, I smashed that window in his office, and it gave him the excuse he wanted to send his new private army after me.
He wants me captured in public. Wants the city to see me as a criminal. And it could work.
Two more police helicopters headed this way and a news chopper, too.
If they get footage... not good. I need to get out of this now.
THERE HE IS.

WHAT ARE HIS POWERS AGAIN?
FILE SAYS HE'S GOT ENHANCED SENSES. INCREDIBLE HEARING, THINGS LIKE THAT.
HEARING? OKAY.

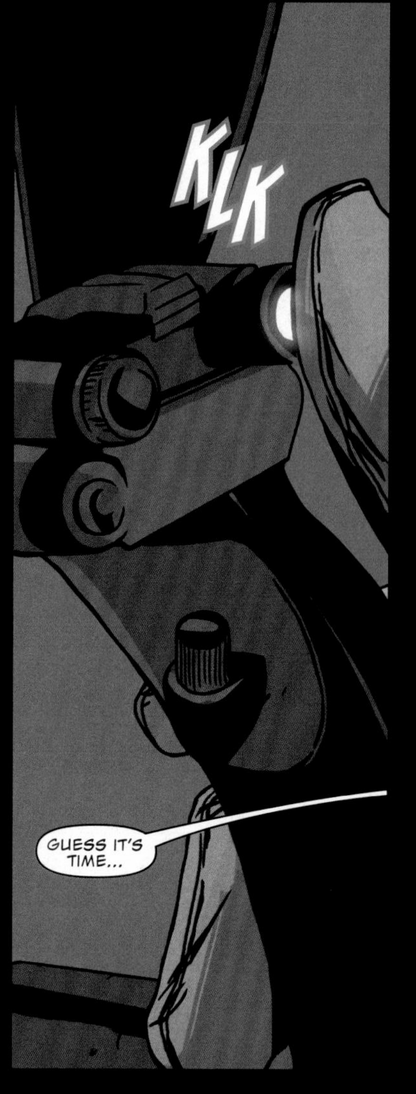
KLK
GUESS IT'S TIME...

...TO ROCK AND ROLL.
BRRRNNNGGGGG

AAGH!
DNNNGGG

NNGAGGH!
KTHD

IT WORKED. HE'S DOWN.
UNCONSCIOUS?
NO. STILL MOVING.

THIS IS ALMOST A SHAME. NEVER WOULD'VE PEGGED DAREDEVIL TO GO BAD, YOU KNOW?
I ALWAYS **LIKED** HIM.
AND THE NEWS IS CATCHING ALL OF THIS, TOO. YEAH...

"...I THINK THIS GUY'S DONE."
FACT CHAN
FC
WHAT WE'RE SEEING HERE IS ABSOLUTELY INCREDIBLE.
THE TARGET OF THE MASSIVE SURGE OF NYPD ACTIVITY TONIGHT SEEMS TO BE THE SUPER HERO KNOWN AS **DAREDEVIL.**

KLK
WELL, IF HE'S STILL MOVING, HE'S NOT DONE YET.
HITTING HIM AGAIN.

NYPD HUNTS DAREDEVIL
FC NEWS channel
DAREDEVIL LOOKS LIKE HE'S BEEN CORNERED BY ONE OF THE NYPD'S SPECIAL PX UNITS, WHICH ARE EQUIPPED TO DEAL WITH ENHANCED HUMANS OF VARIOUS TYPES.
THEY'RE USING SOME KIND OF SONIC CANNON TO SUBDU HIM. INCREDIBLE. IT'S VIBRATIN OUR ENTIRE HELICOPTER, EVE FROM THIS DISTANCE.
NNNNNNGGGHH
HOW IS HE STILL MOVING?
I HAVE NO IDEA. I HAVE THIS THING ON FULL POWER. I'M GOING TO TRY SOMETHING ELSE.
THE PX UNIT HAS SHIFTED TO NON-LETHAL SHOTGUN AMMUNITION, USUALLY KNOWN BY ITS NICKNAME, BEAN BAG ROUNDS.
PFFSH
PFFSH
THESE ARE DESIGNED TO TAKE DOWN A SUSPECT WITHOUT CAUSING SERIOUS INJURY, BUT FROM EVERYTHING WE'VE HEARD...
HUNTS DAREDEVIL
...THEY HURT LIKE HELL.
DAREDEVIL'S STILL UP AND MOVING...
KRCK
ARGH!
BEAUTIFUL.

NEW ATTILAN.
HIGH-SECURITY DETENTION LEVEL.
...BUT HE'S STRUGGLING.
JUST BEAUTIFUL.
EXCUSE ME...GUARD?
STEP BACK FROM THE BARS, MUSE.
BUT I NEED YOU TO HEAR ME. THIS IS IMPORTANT.
FIRST, PLEASE KNOW THAT YOUR HOSPITALITY HERE HAS BEEN WONDERFUL. ART SUPPLIES, TELEVISION, EVEN THE FOOD'S BEEN GOOD.
THE *HUMANITY* YOU INHUMANS SHOW YOUR PRISONERS...IT'S BEYOND REPROACH.
"BUT I'VE FINALLY CHOSEN MY NEXT PROJECT."
SO I'M GOING TO LEAVE NOW.

WHD
GAH!
Damn sonics. Got the dampeners going in my mask...but not fast enough. Feels like my head was... sawn in half.
Getting shot... didn't help... either.
Have to get away, get clear... but they're all over me.
They're not going to stop.
Fisk won't let them stop.
I don't think I can get through this.
KRRS

Not alone.

I'M IN TROUBLE.
I KNOW. WHOLE CITY'S WATCHING. MY TWITTER'S BLOWING UP.
WHY DON'T YOU JUST DITCH THE COSTUME? NO ONE KNOWS WHO YOU ARE. MAYBE GET DOWN INTO THE SEWERS. LOSE THEM DOWN THERE.

LIKE A RAT? IN MY CITY? NO. I WON'T LET HIM DO THAT TO ME. NO.
WE HAD A PLAN FOR SOMETHING LIKE THIS, ONCE.
CAN YOU...
...WILL YOU HELP?

ALL RIGHT.
WHERE WE TALKED ABOUT?
YEAH. THANK Y--
KLK
HNH.

Okay. I can do this. This will work.

Just have to get there.
ALL UNITS! SUSPECT REACQUIRED--HE'S HEADED EAST ON FORTY-SECOND--JUST PASSING FIFTH.
SUSPECT APPROACHING GRAND CENTRAL. GETTING A LITTLE TIGHT IN HERE FOR FLYING, THOUGH--GROUND UNITS, DO YOU HAVE HIM?
WE'RE ON HIM. DAREDEVIL'S GOING FOR THE TUNNEL, NORTHBOUND.
POLICE

ALL UNITS, SUSPECT JUST EMERGED FROM THE PARK AVENUE VIADUCT, UPTOWN SIDE.
CONVERGE AND APPREHEND.
ALL RIGHT. WE GOT THIS GUY.
RADIO CITY
RADIO CITY MUSIC HALL
DAREDEVIL!
GET DOWN HERE, RIGHT NOW! MAKE IT EASY ON YOURSELF!
YOU'VE GOT NOWHERE LEFT TO--
NYPD

RADIO CITY
RADIO CITY MUSIC HALL
Music Hall
WHAT THE HELL?
CAN HE TELEPORT? FILE DIDN'T SAY ANYTHING ABOUT HIM BEING ABLE TO TELEPORT.
--GO!
IT'S DONE.
AND YOU'RE ALL RIGHT? I'M SORRY FOR PUTTING YOU IN THAT POSITION-- I WAS TAKEN BY SURPRISE BY ALL OF THIS, AND--
I'M FINE. TURNED INVISIBLE AND SLIPPED AWAY, JUST LIKE WE PRACTICED.
LISTEN, DAREDEVIL, YOU WANT MY ADVICE...
...WORRY ABOUT YOURSELF.
I'LL STASH THE COSTUME BACK AT THE TRAINING GROUND. SEE YOU AROUND--AND GOOD LUCK WITH ALL THIS.
GUESS NOW THAT DAREDEVIL'S A CRIMINAL, HIS TESTIMONY'S NOT GONNA BE TOO HELPFUL FOR MY ASYLUM CLAIM, HUH?
BLINDSPOT, THIS IS ALL FISK. I PROMISE, ONCE I TAKE HIM DOWN, I'LL--
DON'T PROMISE. DON'T PROMISE ANYTHING...

NEW YORK COUNTY DISTRICT ATTORNEY'S OFFICE. 9A.M.
"...YOU DON'T KNOW HOW TO KEEP THEM."
HEY, MATT.
ELLEN. HOW ARE YOU TODAY?
BETTER THAN YOU, I'M GUESSING. FORGIVE ME FOR SAYING, BUT YOU LOOK EXHAUSTED. YOU OKAY?
I...HAD A LONG NIGHT. JUST NEED TO GET THROUGH THE DAY. WHAT'S UP?
UGH. I HATE TO DO THIS TO YOU, BUT HOCHBERG SENT ME DOWN HERE TO CRACK THE WHIP A LITTLE ON PUTTING TOGETHER A DAREDEVIL INDICTMENT.
HE'S PUBLIC ENEMY NUMBER ONE NOW, ESPECIALLY AFTER LAST NIGHT. ATTACKED THE MAYOR. WHAT THE HELL IS THAT ABOUT?
DAREDEVIL... ATTACKED THE MAYOR?
YEAH. YOU DIDN'T HEAR ABOUT THAT? COPS CHASED HIM HALFWAY ACROSS THE CITY.
I KNOW HE'S A FRIEND OF YOURS. IF YOU CAN, MAYBE TELL HIM TO TURN HIMSELF IN.
BRRNG
I'LL LET YOU GET THAT. BUT SERIOUSLY-- HOCHBERG WANTS SOMETHING SOON.
I KNOW YOU WANT TO DRAG YOUR FEET, BUT I'M NOT SURE THAT'S AN OPTION ANYMORE.
BRRNG

MATT MURDOCK?
YES, THAT'S RIGHT. WHO IS--
PLEASE HOLD FOR THE MAYOR.
MR. MURDOCK.
FISK? WHY THE HELL ARE YOU CALLING ME?
BECAUSE I WOULD LIKE TO MAKE YOU AN OFFER.
THE ANSWER IS--
PLEASE. HEAR ME OUT.
ALL OF YOUR SKEPTICISM-- I UNDERSTAND IT, ESPECIALLY WITH OUR HISTORY. YOU ARE NOT THE ONLY PERSON WHO FEELS THAT WAY ABOUT WILSON FISK SITTING IN CITY HALL.
I WON THE ELECTION, BUT I DID NOT WIN THE CITY. NOT ALL OF IT. NOT ITS HEARTS AND MINDS. THEY WILL COME WITH TIME, BUT IT WILL BE CHALLENGING.
I NEED TO BRING PEOPLE ABOARD MY ADMINISTRATION WHO CAN HELP ME SHOW NEW YORK THAT I AM SINCERE ABOUT MY INTENTIONS.
WHO BETTER THAN THE HERO D.A., MATT MURDOCK, WHO WENT ALL THE WAY TO THE SUPREME COURT AND WON? YOU ARE ABOVE REPROACH.
I, WHETHER IT IS WARRANTED OR NOT, AM NOT. I NEED YOU.
WHAT ARE YOU SAYING, FISK?
I AM SAYING, MR. MURDOCK...
...I WOULD LIKE YOU TO BE MY DEPUTY MAYOR.

SIGN ME UP.

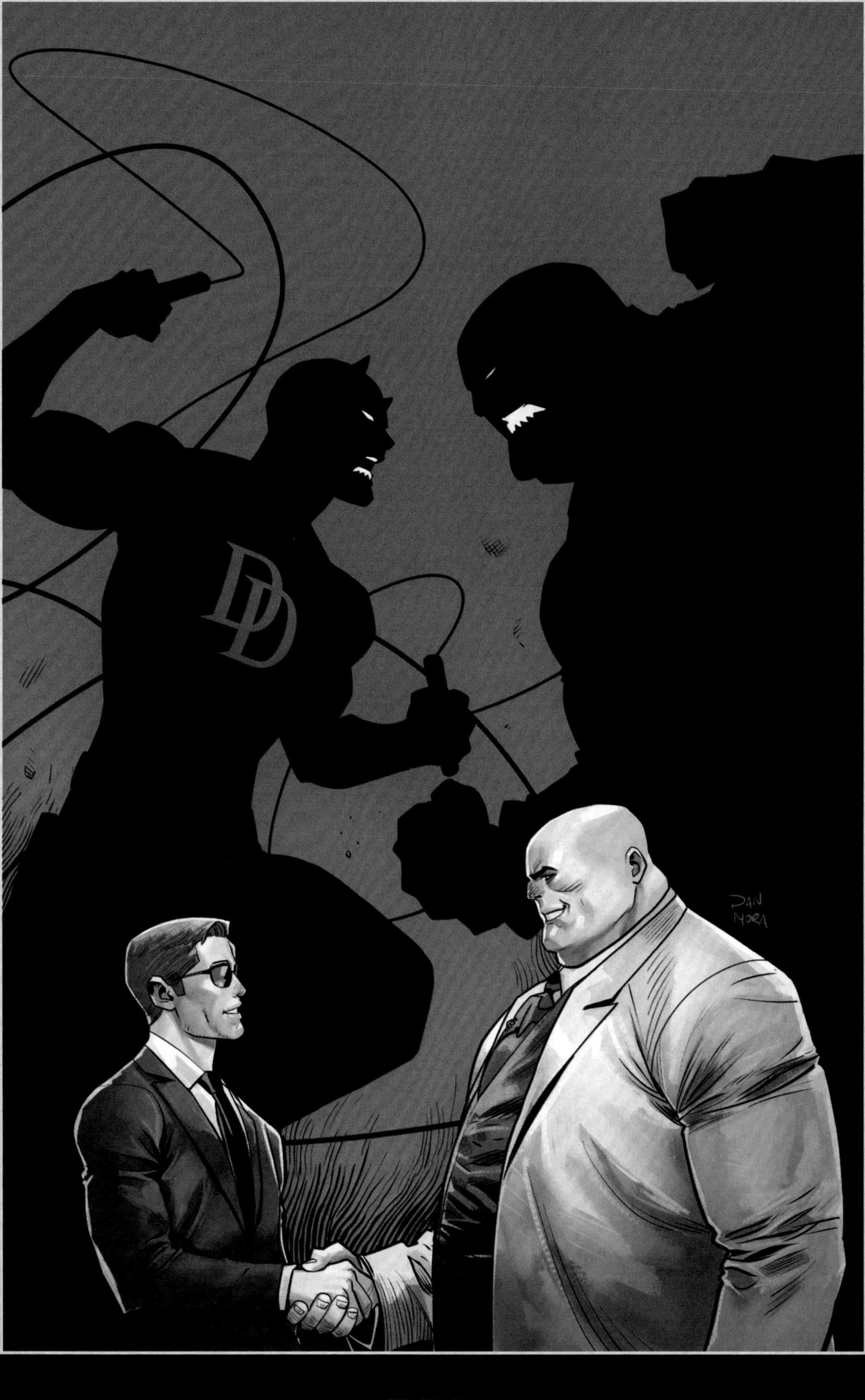

597

NEW YORK CITY HALL.
THE BLUE ROOM.
My name is Matt Murdock.
I am Daredevil.
LET'S GIVE MR. MURDOCK A GOOD OLD-FASHIONED NEW YORK CITY WELCOME!
Wilson Fisk--the Kingpin of Crime--is the mayor of New York.
ILTON
And I just became his right-hand man.

AS FIRST DEPUTY MAYOR, MR. MURDOCK WILL BE RESPONSIBLE FOR ADVISING ME ON A WIDE RANGE OF POLICY ISSUES.
IF IT COMES ACROSS MY DESK, HE'LL SEE IT, AND WE'LL TALK ABOUT IT.
I AM VERY PLEASED MATT AGREED TO JOIN MY ADMINISTRATION.
WHILE HE AND I HAVE HAD OUR DIFFERENCES OVER THE YEARS...

WOULDN'T YOU SAY SO, MR. MURDOCK?
I WOULD, MR. MAYOR.
NEW YORK HAS EIGHT MILLION OPINIONS. I UNDERSTAND THAT, AND I WANT MY CITY TO KNOW THAT I INTEND TO LISTEN TO ALL OF THEM, INCLUDING THOSE IN OPPOSITION TO MINE.
MR. MURDOCK'S APPOINTMENT IS AN EXAMPLE OF THAT, AND IT'S JUST THE BEGINNING.

TIMES SQUARE.
I AM YOUR MAYOR, NEW YORK. BELIEVE IT.
SUUUUUUURE YOU ARE, BIG GUY SURE.
MATT...WHAT THE HELL ARE YOU DOING?

STATEN ISLAND.
...I THINK WE CAN BOTH AGREE THAT NEW YORK CITY IS THE MOST WONDERFUL PLACE IN THE WORLD.
HNH.
FC NEWS

NOW, I THINK PERHAPS THE NEW DEPUTY MAYOR CAN ANSWER A FEW OF YOUR QUESTIONS.
MR. MURDOCK! TO YOUR LEFT, NEAR THE FRONT!
MR. MURDOCK!

THANK YOU, MR. MURDOCK. GEORGE GASTINEAUX, FROM THE TIMES.
I HAVE TO SAY, THIS COMES AS A SURPRISE. YOU'VE BEEN AN OUTSPOKEN CRITIC OF MR. FISK SINCE THE BEGINNING OF YOUR LEGAL CAREER.
NOW YOU WANT TO HELP HIM RUN THE CITY? I HAVE TO ASK... WHY?
WELL, GEORGE, YOU KNOW WHAT THEY SAY...

"...BETTER THE DEVIL YOU KNOW."
THAT WENT WELL, I THINK.
HOW DO YOU WANT TO GET STARTED, WILSON? WE CAN RUN THROUGH SOME OF THE BIGGER ISSUES NOW.
OR WOULD YOU RATHER I JUST SIT IN YOUR OFFICE AND LISTEN, ABSORB THINGS FOR A WHILE?
UH...
...WILSON?
HI, MR. MURDOCK, MY NAME'S STEVE.
I'M SUPPOSED TO SHOW YOU TO YOUR OFFICE.

IT'S JUST UP HERE.
HERE WE ARE. IT'S ACTUALLY PRETTY NICE!
I'LL HAVE TO TAKE YOUR WORD FOR IT, STEVE.
OH, YEAH. OF COURSE.
THEY SET UP A PHONE IN HERE YET? WE'LL HAVE TO MAKE A FEW ACCOMMODATIONS BECAUSE I'M, YOU KNOW, BLIND, BUT I'VE BEEN THROUGH THIS BEFORE.
I CAN GIVE YOU A LIST OF THE THINGS I NEED.
SURE THING, MR. MURDOCK.
HM.
WHAT ARE THESE?
BRIEFING BOOKS. THE MAYOR HAD ME BRING THEM UP FOR YOU. CITY POLICY, REGULATIONS, PENDING ISSUES FROM THE LAST ADMINISTRATION.
THERE'S... KIND OF A LOT.
AH.
NOT TO BELABOR THE POINT, STEVE...
...BUT YOU DID HEAR ME SAY I'M *BLIND*, RIGHT?

I MEAN, YEAH. OBVIOUSLY.
ARE THESE IN BRAILLE?
NOPE.
SO HOW...

DON'T WORRY, MR. MURDOCK. I GOT YOU.
THEY SAID I'M SUPPOSED TO READ THEM TO YOU.

ALL OF THEM?
YEAH. I KNOW WHAT YOU MEAN. MIGHT TAKE A WHILE.
OH, WELL.

OKAY. THIS FIRST ONE'S RECENTLY ADOPTED CITY RULES AND REGULATIONS, WITH THE TITLES AND TEXT.
"INCLUSIONARY HOUSING AND 421-A AFFORDABLE UNITS."

"THE RULE AMENDMENTS TO CHAPTER 41 OF TITLE 28 OF THE RULES OF THE CITY OF NEW YORK WOULD LIMIT THE ZONING BONUS GENERATED BY..."
Have to hand it to you, Fisk. This is actually pretty clever.

KNOCK KNOCK. HOPE I'M NOT INTERRUPTING.
Oh, thank *God.*
UH...WE'RE ACTUALLY PRETTY BUSY.
AND YOU ARE...?
WE'RE GOOD, STEVE. THIS IS FOGGY NELSON, AN OLD FRIEND OF MINE. I'LL NEED THE ROOM, PLEASE.
WHATEVER YOU SAY, SIR. I'M AT EXTENSION 4518. CALL ME WHEN YOU'RE DONE AND WE'LL GET BACK TO WORK.
SEEMS LIKE A GOOD KID.
WELL, HE SEEMS TO ENJOY READING, I'LL GIVE HIM THAT.
WHAT CAN I DO FOR YOU, FOGGY? WHAT ARE YOU DOING HERE?
NO, MATT.
WHAT ARE *YOU* DOING HERE?

IT'S RUDE TO POINT.
HOW'D YOU GET IN HERE, ANYWAY? I WOULD HAVE THOUGHT CITY HALL HAD PRETTY GOOD SECURITY.
COME ON. I'M ALMOST AS FAMOUS AS YOU ARE. EVERYONE KNOWS FOGGY NELSON, EVEN IN CITY HALL. I'M CHARMING AND HARMLESS. PEOPLE JUST WAVE ME IN.
LOOK, CAN WE JUST CUT TO THE CHASE?
MY FIRST THOUGHT WHEN I HEARD ABOUT THIS DEPUTY MAYOR STUFF WAS THAT YOU WERE PLANNING TO KILL THE KINGPIN AND TAKE OVER THE CITY.
BUT THEN I LOOKED UP THE RULES OF SUCCESSION, AND--
YUP. DEPUTY MAYOR DOESN'T TAKE OVER IF THE REGULAR MAYOR'S INCAPACITATED. IT'S THE PUBLIC ADVOCATE. I NEVER GET TO BE MAYOR.
YOU WANT TO KNOW WHY?

DEPUTY MAYOR ISN'T AN ELECTED OFFICE.
FIORELLO LaGUARDIA CREATED THE POSITION BACK IN THE 1940s SO HE'D HAVE SOMEONE TO GO TO PARTIES AND ATTEND CEREMONIES FOR HIM.
BACK THEN, IT WAS JUST A FIGUREHEAD THING.
SEEMS LIKE IT STILL IS, BUDDY.
THERE'S *NO WAY* FISK LETS YOU NEAR ANY ACTUAL POLICY.

I JUST DON'T GET IT. YOU WERE A HERO IN THE D.A.'S OFFICE! YOU COULD HAVE MADE A REAL DIFFERENCE.
NO. FISK FORCED HOCHBERG TO START BUILDING CASES AGAINST THE CITY'S STREET-LEVEL HEROES. SPIDER-MAN, IRON FIST, LUKE CAGE. ALL OF THEM.
DAREDEVIL, TOO. THAT WAS MY ASSIGNMENT, ACTUALLY. THE D.A.'S OFFICE WAS A DEAD-END FOR ME.
OKAY, FINE. BACK TO PRIVATE PRACTICE, THEN. JUST...ANYTHING BUT THIS. YOU'VE...YOU'VE NEUTERED YOURSELF! YOU CAN'T DO ANYTHING IN HERE!
MAYBE MATT MURDOCK CAN'T.
BUT DAREDEVIL CAN.
FISK'S GOING TO START DOING TERRIBLE THINGS TO THIS CITY. HE HAS TO. HE'S THE KINGPIN. AND WHEN HE DOES, I'LL KNOW.
HE CAN USE ME FOR WHATEVER P.R. BUMP HE WANTS. I DON'T CARE. HE BROUGHT THE DEVIL INTO HIS HOUSE, AND THE DEVIL IS LISTENING.
DAREDEVIL'S IN TROUBLE, TOO, THOUGH. THE COPS PUT OUT A REWARD FOR HIS CAPTURE. DID YOU KNOW THAT?
EVEN IF YOU DO HEAR SOMETHING, WHAT THEN?
EH, I'LL PLAY IT BY EAR.
UGH. TERRIBLE.
I... DAMMIT. HOW CAN I HELP?
NOTHING RIGHT NOW. BUT WHEN I NEED YOU, I'LL CALL.
THANK YOU, FOGGY...IT'S NICE TO KNOW SOMEONE'S OUT THERE WORRYING ABOUT ME.
LIKE YOU GIVE ME ANY CHOICE.
OKAY. JUST BE CAREFUL. IF THERE'S ANYTHING I KNOW ABOUT WILSON FISK--IT'S THAT IF YOU THINK YOU'RE PLAYING HIM...
...HE IS DEFINITELY PLAYING YOU.

I know what people think of me.
Those little things people say about me after they leave the room...
BE CAREFUL, MATT.
I hear it all.
I MEAN IT.
WHAT WAS THAT?
NOTHING, STEVE. GO ON IN. HE'S WAITING FOR YOU.
Good...
WE GIVE HIM JUST ENOUGH TO MAKE HIM THINK HE HAS A CHANCE TO INFLUENCE ME.
TO THINK HE MIGHT BE ABLE TO...MAKE THINGS BETTER.
NEW YORK STATE
NOTHING WILL STOP ME FROM DOING WHAT NEEDS TO BE DONE FOR THIS CITY.
Getting faint. He must be moving. I'm gonna lose him in a second.
WITH THAT IN MIND--I WANT A PROGRESS REPORT ON THE SARNOS PROJECT, WESLEY.
OF COURSE, MR. FISK. RIGHT NOW, WE'RE--

...and bad.
MURDOCK IS NOTHING.
ARE YOU SURE, SIR? HE'S BEEN PRETTY TENACIOUS IN THE PAST. JUST BECAUSE HE AGREED TO WORK WITH YOU DOESN'T MEAN HE'S ON YOUR SIDE.
I DON'T THINK HE'S ON MY SIDE, WESLEY. BUT WHILE HE'S HERE, WE CAN KEEP HIM TILTING AT ANY NUMBER OF WINDMILLS.
WE WILL POINT HIM IN WHATEVER DIRECTION WE CHOOSE. HE WILL SPEND ALL HIS ENERGY ON LOST CAUSES AND MANUFACTURED ISSUES.
HE WILL BE DOING *THAT*, WHICH MEANS HE WILL NOT BE WORKING AGAINST ME IN THE WIDER WORLD.
HI AGAIN. SO...MR. NELSON'S GONE.
READY TO GET BACK TO READING?
Damn you, Steve.
ALL RIGHT. NOW WHERE WERE WE?
Still... the *Sarnos* project.
It's a start.

HELL'S KITCHEN.
This is probably a bad idea.
The NYPD's still looking for me, and I'm not sure Blindspot will be willing to bail me out again.
I should lie low for a while. Work on Fisk from inside City Hall
Sarnos. There's something there. I know it.
I don't need to go on patrol tonight.
I shouldn't do this.
But if I'm not on the streets, the Kingpin wins.
The Kingpin will not win.

Still, no need to be stupid here.
I'll stay up high-- harder to spot from the street.
Let my senses tell me where I need to be.

Ah.
EVERYTHING IN THE REGISTER! NOW!

Perfect.

HURRY UP, MAN! WHAT'S TAKING SO LONG?
I'M TRYING! YOU'RE POINTING GUNS, OKAY? MAKES ME NERVOUS!
GONNA BE SHOOTING THESE GUNS, YOU DON'T GET US THAT MONEY!

NO1 CANS
125
NO. NO ONE'S GETTING SHOT TODAY.
HEY... YOU'RE *DAREDEVIL*, RIGHT?
YEAH. AND YOU KNOW WHAT WILL HAPPEN IF YOU DON'T DROP THOSE GUNS.
IF WE *DON'T* DROP THESE GUNS? YEAH, I KNOW WHAT.
BNG BNG
Huh.
SHHK
KRCK
K-KRCK
Can't say I didn't warn them.

YOU ALL RIGHT?
Y-YES. I AM OKAY.
GOOD. CALL THE POLICE TO COME GET THESE GUYS BEFORE THEY WAKE UP.
CAN YOU BELIEVE THOSE YS JUST STARTED SHOOTING LIKE THAT? AT ME?
NOT LIKE HOLDING UP A BODEGA'S ALL THAT SMART TO BEGIN WITH, BUT MAN. IT'S LIKE THEY WEREN'T THINKING AT ALL.
OH, DON'T HOLD IT AGAINST THEM, MR. DAREDEVIL...
...MAYBE THEY JUST WANTED THE REWARD.
DO NOT MOVE. I PRESSED THE ALARM. POLICE ARE ON THE WAY.
COME ON, MAN. HOW MANY ROBBERIES HAVE I STOPPED IN THIS PLACE OVER THE YEARS?
MANY. BUT TIMES CHANGE, AND THE REWARD IS VERY BIG.
FREEZE! DOWN ON THE GR--
AGH!
WHAT THE HELL?
What...what's happening?

HEY THERE, DAREDEVIL.
REMEMBER ME?
Frank McGee. Yeah, I remember.
Used to be an NYPD detective, now he's the head of security for New Attilan.
CAN'T... CAN'T SEE.
DON'T WORRY, FOLKS. IT'S NOT PERMANENT.
IT'LL CLEAR UP. JUST BLINK A LOT.
He can generate blasts of light from his eyes, like a camera flash.
Supposed to be very intense. Must be how he shut down those cops.
He's Inhuman.

HEY, RED.
UNLESS YOU'RE WAITING ON AN EGG AND CHEESE OR SOMETHING, I'D LOVE TO CHAT WITH YOU OUTSIDE.
Frank brought an entire New Attilan security squad. Even a few of the royal guards. This seems...serious.
WHAT ARE YOU DOING HERE, FRANK?
NOT EVEN A "THANK YOU"? I JUST SAVED YOUR ASS.
GET IN.
LET'S GO FOR A RIDE.

I'VE BEEN LOOKING FOR YOU.
WHY DIDN'T YOU JUST CALL MURDOCK? HE KNOWS HOW TO REACH ME.
I FIGURED YOU TWO WERE ON THE OUTS, WHAT WITH MAYOR FISK CALLING FOR YOUR HEAD, AND THEN MURDOCK SIGNING UP TO BE THE DEPUTY MAYOR.
CAN'T REALLY FIGURE THAT, HONESTLY.
WE'RE FINE. NEXT TIME YOU NEED ME, JUST GET IN TOUCH WITH HIM.
WELL, THIS WAY WORKED, TOO. YOU MIGHT NOT KNOW THIS, BUT NEW ATTILAN MONITORS ALL RADIO AND WIRELESS TRAFFIC IN NEW YORK CITY.
KEEPING AN EYE ON THE NEIGHBORS.
SO WHEN THE CALL CAME OVER THE POLICE BANDS ABOUT DAREDEVIL POPPING UP IN A BODEGA IN HELL'S KITCHEN, WELL, HEY.
WE ZIPPED RIGHT OVER. EASY AS--
STOP STALLING. YOU RISKED A MAJOR DIPLOMATIC INCIDENT COMING INTO THE CITY LIKE THIS.
YOU MUST NEED SOMETHING IMPORTANT. WHAT IS IT?
ALL RIGHT, LOOK. YOU HELPED ME OUT BEFORE. I WANT TO PAY THAT BACK. WANTED TO GIVE YOU THE HEADS-UP.
TELL ME, FRANK.
YOU REMEMBER MUSE?

The serial killer who turns his victims into *art?*
The creature who ripped out Blindspot's eyes and broke his mind?
The worst monster to pop up in my life in a very long time?
YEAH. I REMEMBER MUSE.
YOU TOOK HIM INTO CUSTODY. SAID NO ONE WOULD EVER HAVE TO WORRY ABOUT HIM AGAIN. SAID YOU'D PUT HIM IN THE DEEPEST CELL YOU COULD FIND ON NEW ATTILAN.
YEAH, WELL, I DID, AND THEN HE GOT OUT.
KILLED TWELVE OF MY MEN ON THE WAY, TOO. TWELVE.
Oh, no. *Sam.*
YEAH?
BLINDSPOT. LISTEN TO ME. I DON'T KNOW HOW, BUT MUSE *ESCAPED.* HE'S LOOSE.
I DON'T KNOW WHERE HE IS, BUT HE...HE MIGHT BE *COMING* FOR YOU. YOU NEED TO--
Don't be too late. Don't be too late.
THAT'S WHY I WASN'T TOO KEEN ON YOU GETTING TOSSED IN JAIL. I WANT YOU FREE, OUT ON THE STREETS.
WE'RE LOOKING FOR HIM TOO, BUT YOU FOUND HIM LAST TIME--MAYBE YOU CAN DO IT AGAIN.
YOU DO, CALL ME. I'LL COME.
OH. YEAH. I DON'T KNOW WHERE HE IS, EITHER.

BUT I'M PRETTY SURE I KNOW WHERE HE *WAS.*
I AM NOT A CROOK

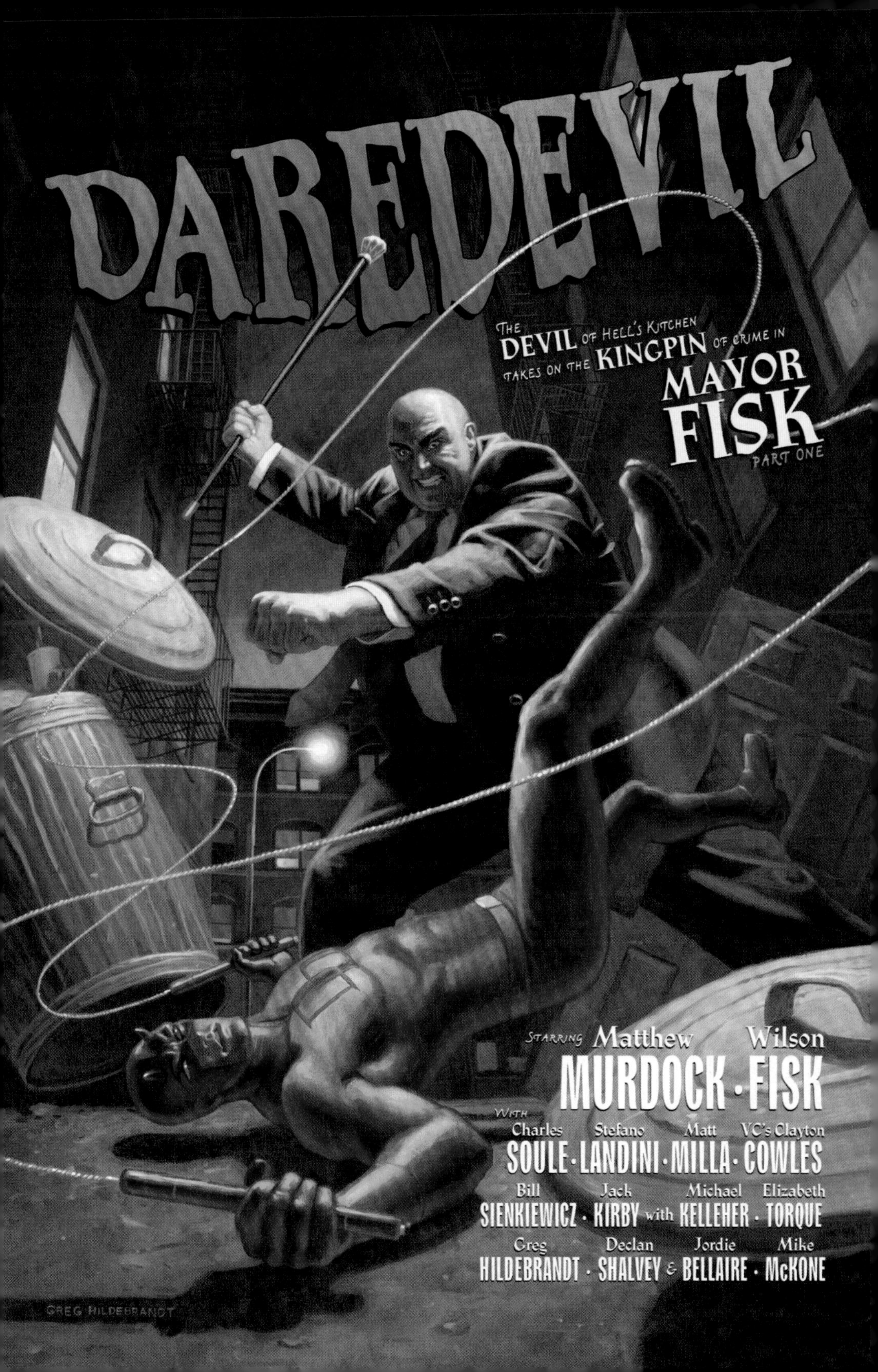

DAREDEVIL

THE DEVIL OF HELL'S KITCHEN TAKES ON THE KINGPIN OF CRIME IN

MAYOR FISK

PART ONE

STARRING Matthew MURDOCK · Wilson FISK

WITH

Charles SOULE · Stefano LANDINI · Matt MILLA · VC's Clayton COWLES

Bill SIENKIEWICZ · Jack KIRBY with Michael KELLEHER · Elizabeth TORQUE

Greg HILDEBRANDT · Declan SHALVEY & Jordie BELLAIRE · Mike McKONE

GREG HILDEBRANDT

DAN MORA

ANOTHER PIECE BY THE STREET ARTIST KNOWN AS MUSE APPEARED LAST NIGHT ON THE JACOB K. JAVITS BUILDING AT 26 FEDERAL PLAZA.
IN KEEPING WITH THE THEME OF PREVIOUS WORKS, THE NEW MURAL FEATURES ONE OF NEW YORK'S LONGTIME COSTUMED VIGILANTES.
NYC ONE
5 VIGILANTES AS POP ART
"THIS TIME, IT'S SPIDER-MAN, SHOWN GIVING A THUMBS-UP.
"OR, POSSIBLY, A THUMBS-DOWN, DEPENDING ON YOUR POINT OF VIEW.
SPIDERS ARE PEOPLE
100
"AUTHORITIES ARE AT A LOSS TO EXPLAIN HOW SUCH A LARGE MURAL COULD HAVE BEEN CREATED OVERNIGHT ON ONE OF THE CITY'S MOST HIGHLY SECURED BUILDINGS.
"IT HAS THAT IN COMMON WITH THE OTHER MUSE WORKS THAT HAVE CAPTIVATED THE CITY, ALL OF WHICH FEATURE NEW YORK'S WELL-KNOWN COSTUMED CRIMEFIGHTERS.

UKE CAGE.
DO BE
AFRAID
OF ME
"IRON FIST.
I
can
do
ANYTHIN
I

AND OF COURSE, THE FIRST PIECE TO APPEAR-- DAREDEVIL, ON THE MANHATTAN MUNICIPAL BUILDING.
THESE WORKS SEEM DESIGNED TO ACT AS A COUNTERPOINT TO NEWLY ELECTED MAYOR WILSON FISK'S STANCE AGAINST COSTUMED VIGILANTES.
THEY INVITE SYMPATHY--OR AT LEAST PROVIDE A DIFFERENT POINT OF VIEW.
GREEN IS CLEAN
5 VIGILANTES AS POP ART

IF WE COULD ASK THE ARTIST, WE MIGHT KNOW MORE ABOUT THEIR INTENTIONS--BUT SO FAR, THIS PERSON HASN'T REVEALED HIS OR HER IDENTITY.
ALL WE HAVE IS ONE WORD--THE SAME SIGNATURE ON EVERY MURAL--LEAVING NEW YORK CITY ASKING...
GREEN IS CLEAN
5 VIGILANTES AS POP ART

"MOON KNIGHT.
I'M NOT CRAZY I'M AWAKE
GREEN IS CLEAN
"JENNIFER WALTERS, ALSO KNOWN AS SHE-HULK."
WHO IS THIS MUSE?

I'M NOT SURE I QUITE AGREE WITH HIS...
...ARTISTIC POINT OF VIEW.
I THINK I WOULD LIKE TO MEET HIM.
CITY HALL.
OFFICE OF THE MAYOR.
YOU AND EVERYONE ELSE IN THIS CITY, MR. FISK. I HATE TO SAY IT, BUT WE DON'T HAVE ANY IDEA WHO THIS GUY IS.
WE DON'T EVEN KNOW WHAT HE'S USING TO PAINT THESE MURALS. THE SANITATION DEPARTMENT CAN'T MAKE A DENT IN IT SO FAR.

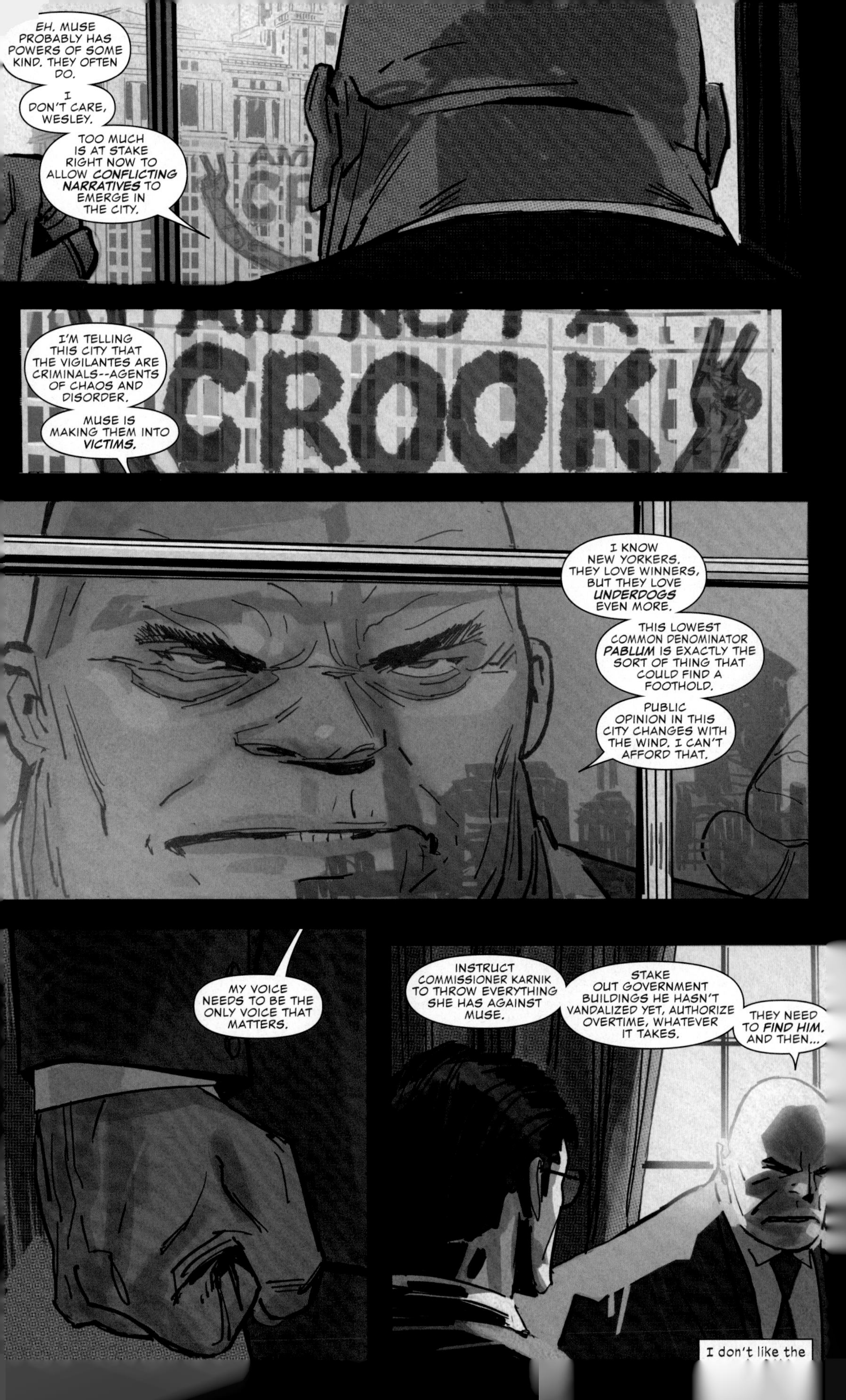
EH. MUSE PROBABLY HAS POWERS OF SOME KIND. THEY OFTEN DO.
I DON'T CARE, WESLEY.
TOO MUCH IS AT STAKE RIGHT NOW TO ALLOW CONFLICTING NARRATIVES TO EMERGE IN THE CITY.
I'M TELLING THIS CITY THAT THE VIGILANTES ARE CRIMINALS--AGENTS OF CHAOS AND DISORDER.
MUSE IS MAKING THEM INTO VICTIMS.
CROOK
I KNOW NEW YORKERS. THEY LOVE WINNERS, BUT THEY LOVE UNDERDOGS EVEN MORE.
THIS LOWEST COMMON DENOMINATOR PABLUM IS EXACTLY THE SORT OF THING THAT COULD FIND A FOOTHOLD.
PUBLIC OPINION IN THIS CITY CHANGES WITH THE WIND. I CAN'T AFFORD THAT.
MY VOICE NEEDS TO BE THE ONLY VOICE THAT MATTERS.
INSTRUCT COMMISSIONER KARNIK TO THROW EVERYTHING SHE HAS AGAINST MUSE.
STAKE OUT GOVERNMENT BUILDINGS HE HASN'T VANDALIZED YET, AUTHORIZE OVERTIME, WHATEVER IT TAKES.
THEY NEED TO FIND HIM. AND THEN...
I don't like the

OFFICE OF THE DEPUTY MAYOR.
...I WANT MUSE'S ARTISTIC ASPIRATIONS TO DIE ON THE VINE.
Fisk has no idea what he's dealing with.
...THAT'S IT FOR DEPARTMENT OF HEALTH AND MENTAL HYGIENE, MR. MURDOCK.
I need to get up there--try to convince him that he needs to be careful with Muse.
YOU WANT TO MOVE ON TO THE NEXT ONE, OR DO YOU WANT TO TAKE A BREAK?
NO PROBLEM, MR. FISK. I'LL REACH OUT AS SOON AS WE'RE DONE HERE.
Can't go up there too soon, though--he could figure I've got his office bugged or something.
Which I do, basically, except *I'm* the--
MR. MURDOCK?
GAH!
OH, I'M SORRY, MR. MURDOCK. DIDN'T MEAN TO GRAB YOU LIKE THAT.
YOU WEREN'T ANSWERING. I THOUGHT MAYBE... MAYBE YOU FELL ASLEEP.

FELL ASLEEP? COME ON, STEVE. I'M EXTREMELY FOCUSED.
OKAY, COOL. I WAS THINKING WE'D TAKE A BREAK BEFORE WE START THE NEXT BINDER--BUT SOUNDS LIKE YOU'RE GOOD TO GO.

WHOA-- THIS SHOULD BE A GOOD ONE.
IT'S ALL THE REGULATIONS AND POLICY CHANGES THE LAST FEW MAYORS PUT INTO PLACE--THE WAYS THEY TWEAKED THINGS TO MAKE CITY HALL RUN THE WAY THEY WANTED.
All right, Matt. Tune Steve out. You know the timbre of his voice.
A LOT OF THIS IS STILL IN EFFECT, ACTUALLY. IN FACT...
Find it, isolate it... tune it out.
...SOME OF THIS APPLIES DIRECTLY TO YOU.
Perfect. And now...

...time to really listen.
...ALL GOOD WITH THE COMMISSIONER, SIR. SHE SAYS SHE'S ON BOARD--ALL HANDS ON DECK TO BRING IN MUSE.
GOOD. LET'S TURN TO THE SARNOS PROJECT, WESLEY.

I'VE SET MEETINGS ALL AFTERNOON. HEADED TO THE FIRST ONE NOW, ACTUALLY.
I THINK EVERYONE'S ON BOARD.
MAKE IT EXTREMELY CLEAR TO THEM. THIS IS THE ONLY WAY FORWARD.
TIMES HAVE CHANGED. THE OLD WAYS ARE OVER.
SELL THEM ON THE *POTENTIAL.*
ABSOLUTELY, MR. MAYOR. SHOULDN'T BE A PROBLEM.
YOU KNOW ME. I COULD SELL A UNICYCLE TO A--

NNF!

MATT! I DIDN'T SEE YOU THERE.
MUTUAL.

I SHOULD GET YOU A LITTLE BELL, SO I ALWAYS KNOW WHERE YOU ARE.
I CAN MAKE THAT HAPPEN, RIGHT? I'M THE ALL-POWERFUL DEPUTY MAYOR, AFTER ALL.
UH, I DON'T...

I'M JOKING, WESLEY. I'M FINE. WHEN YOU'RE BLIND, YOU GET USED TO FALLING DOWN.
DOESN'T MEAN I'M IN THE MARKET FOR A *UNICYCLE*, THOUGH.
RUN ALONG, NOW. MAYOR TYPES NEED TO CHAT.

MR. MAYOR.
MR. MURDOCK.

I FIND IT HARD TO BELIEVE YOU'VE ALREADY GOTTEN THROUGH ALL THE BRIEFING BOOKS I HAD SENT DOWN.
I HAVEN'T. STEVE'S MAKING PROGRESS, BUT THERE'S A LOT OF MATERIAL.
I NEED YOU TO KNOW THOSE REGULATIONS BACKWARDS AND FORWARDS IF YOU'RE GOING TO HELP ME RUN THIS CITY. EVERYTHING ELSE TAKES SECOND PLACE.
DO *YOU* KNOW THEM?
NO. THAT'S WHY I HIRED YOU.
WHAT DO YOU WANT? I HAVE WORK TO DO.
I STILL HAVE A LOT OF FRIENDS IN THE NYPD. THE D.A.'S OFFICE AND THE COPS WORK HAND IN HAND. SO, I HEARD ABOUT THE PUSH TO TRY TO CATCH THIS ARTIST-- MUSE.
THAT JUST HAPPENED. THEY MUST BE VERY GOOD FRIENDS OF YOURS.
THEY ARE. I CAME UP HERE TO TELL YOU, THOUGH... I THINK IT'S A BAD IDEA.
MUSE ISN'T JUST SOME KID WITH SOME SPRAY PAINT. HE'S ***EXTREMELY DANGEROUS.***
YOU REMEMBER THAT SERIAL KILLER OPERATING IN THE CITY A LITTLE WHILE BACK? TABLOIDS CALLED HIM VINCENT VAN GORE.
THAT'S MUSE. SAME GUY.

YOU DON'T WANT TO SEND THE COPS AFTER HIM UNPREPARED. N FACT, MAYBE DON'T SEND THEM AFTER HIM AT ALL.
HOW DO YOU KNOW ALL OF THIS?
I...
YOUR FRIEND DAREDEVIL.
YES. HE'S FOUGHT MUSE. THAT'S HOW I KNOW HOW DEADLY HE CAN BE.
THERE ARE PEOPLE OUT THERE WHO CAN HANDLE THIS. I KNOW YOUR PUBLIC STANCE ON THE COSTUMES, BUT--
PEOPLE. LIKE DAREDEVIL. THE DEFENDERS. SPIDER-MAN. PEOPLE LIKE THAT.
YOU'RE IN CONTACT WITH THEM?
I COULD BE.
BACK-CHANNEL.
NO ONE WOULD NEED TO KNOW.
NO, MR. MURDOCK.
THE ANSWER IS NO, AND THE NEXT TIME YOU BRING ME A SUGGESTION LIKE THIS I'LL HAVE YOU INDICTED ON CONSPIRACY CHARGES. THEY ARE CRIMINALS.
PEOPLE ARE GOING TO DIE, FISK.
PEOPLE DIE EVERY DAY.

That took longer than I wanted.
Wesley's probably long gone by now. I should have--
EEEE
Wait.
EEEE
There it is.
The little bell.
EEEE

trasonic bug. Slipped it in his pocket when he knocked me down.
Super-high frequency. Maybe dogs can pick it up...and me, of course.
I can hear it...and I can follow it.
Poor guy had no idea at all.
Almost feel sorry for him.
Almost.
Back in black.
Harder to see against the city backdrop than the red costume.
I don't like the idea that Daredevil has to *hide*, but after that disaster in the bodega, and the reward out for me...
I can be dumb, but I try not to be ***stupid***.
No sirens. No shouts from the sidewalk. That's a good sign.
I think I'm okay.
Now... Wesley...

...let's see what you're up to.
LITTLE ITALY.
WHAT THE HELL IS THIS?
A LIST OF ALL THE POSITIONS IN CITY GOVERNMENT THE MAYOR GETS TO APPOINT.
THINK OF IT LIKE A MENU, HAMMERHEAD.

THERE'S ABOUT FIFTY DIFFERENT DEPARTMENTS. EDUCATION, ENVIRONMENTAL PROTECTION, SANITATION, TRANSPORTATION... YOU NAME IT.
FISK LIKES YOU FOR CORRECTIONS.
PRISONS? I AIN'T NO KINDA FAN OF PRISONS.
YEAH? HOW ABOUT MONEY? HEAD OF CORRECTIONS GETS TO ASSIGN THOSE FAT PRISON CONTRACTS, NOT TO MENTION ALL THE CASH YOU CAN MAKE ON THE SIDE.
THERE'RE POSSIBILITIES HERE. IF YOU DON'T TAKE IT, SOMEONE ELSE SURE AS HELL WILL.

WAIT...YOU TALKING TO OTHER PEOPLE ABOUT THIS?

OH, YEAH.

SOHO.
THE MAYOR THINKS YOU'D BE GREAT TO RUN THE DEPARTMENT OF EDUCATION, FELICIA.
LUCKY ME. SHAPING THE MINDS OF THE CITY'S YOUTH.
MIDTOWN.
DEPARTMENT OF AGING, EH? STEREOTYPICAL, BUT IT COULD WORK.
YES. IT COULD WORK FOR THE OWL.
HARLEM.
I WANT TO BE THE POLICE COMMISSIONER.
MAYBE A LITTLE EARLY FOR THAT, DIAMONDBACK... BUT WE'LL SEE WHAT HAPPENS.
ANYTHING'S POSSIBLE. FISK WANTS TO HEAR FROM EVERYONE. YOU'LL ALL HAVE A CHANCE TO MAKE YOUR CASE. YOU KNOW THE MEET?
SARNOS. UP IN THE BRONX. SATURDAY NIGHT. YEAH, I KNOW.
WELL, SHOW UP. ANYONE WHO'S NOT THERE DOESN'T GET A PIECE. YOU DON'T WANT TO BE ON THE OUTSIDE.
THIS IS THE FUTURE OF NEW YORK CITY.
Not if I can help it.
A few days until they all meet. That's good.

THE MEATPACKIN
DISTRIC
YOU LOVE ME?
YOU LOVE WHAT
I DO
MUSE
Should be enough time to deal with Muse.
EXCUSE ME...BUT ARE YOU ACTUALLY HIM?

ARE YOU ACTUALLY MUSE?
I JUST SIGNED MY NAME TO THIS PIECE, DIDN'T I? I WOULD NEVER TAKE CREDIT FOR SOMEONE ELSE'S WORK. THAT'S A CRIME.
OH, WOW. DO YOU MIND IF WE...CAN WE GET A PICTURE WITH YOU?

MY PLEASURE.

WAIT. THIS LOOKS WEIRD.
I DON'T THINK IT WORKED.
YOU'RE PRETTY.
WHAT... UH...THANK YOU.

YOU'RE PRETTY.
YOU'RE PRETTY.
YOU'RE PRETTY.
YOU'RE PRETTY.
YOU'RE PRETTY.
YOU'RE PRETTY.
STOP SAYING THAT!

I CAN MAKE YOU BEAUTIFUL.

DOWN ON THE GROUND! NOW!
OH, LADIES. I'M SORRY.
ANOTHER TIME, MAYBE.
I WON'T TELL YOU AGAIN!
I HEARD YOU. I JUST DON'T WANT TO GET DOWN ON THE GROUND.
IT'S FILTHY.
BNG
KRCK
RRIP
AGH!

SEE?
JUST FILTHY.
HMMM.
YOU KNOW, FRANK, I ACTUALLY THINK THIS IS BETTER.
REALLY GIVES THE PIECE SOME OOMPH.
HNH.
THEY HAVEN'T FOUND ANYTHING YET, SIR.
SIX OFFICERS DEAD, AND NO TRACES AT ALL. IT'S...VERY STRANGE.
YES. IT IS. THESE WERE GOOD MEN, JUST DOING THEIR JOBS.

NUSE
A TRAGEDY.
WE CAN USE THAT.

Find it.
Find the void.
I know how to do this. I've done it before. Muse pulls sensory data to himself like a vortex.
Reach out across the city. Look for the place with no sounds, no scents... nothing.
Find the--

MURDOCK.
No. Put Fisk aside.

Put aside what he's doing to the city.
There's time for Fisk later. I have a plan for Fisk.
Focus on *Muse.*

He killed six police officers--the SoHo Six, the tabloids are calling them.
MUSE
Muse killed them...but then Fisk *used* it.

He blamed it on the *Punisher.*
The cops were killed near a mural Muse created with Castle's face on it. That was all the evidence Fisk needed.

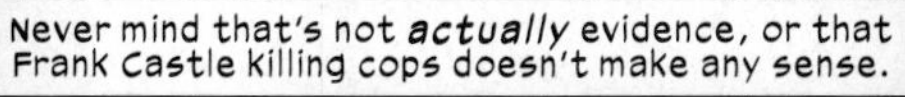

Never mind that's not *actually* evidence, or that Frank Castle killing cops doesn't make any sense.

People ate it up. He's been telling people the costumes are dangerous criminals ever since he got elected, and now...proof.
NO VIGILANTES FOR NYC
FISK RULES
JUSTICE FOR THE SOHO SIX
FISK RULES
JUSTICE FOR THE SOHO SIX
Or...close enough for Wilson Fisk. The truth is whatever people believe.
Not everyone--New York City never completely agrees on *anything*--but enough. And now--

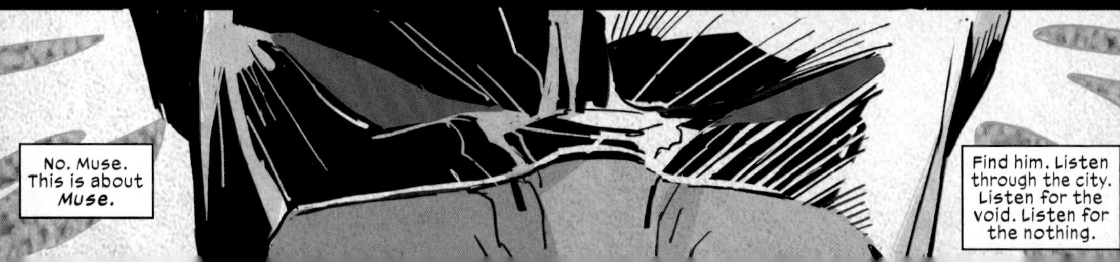

No. Muse. This is about *Muse.*
Find him. Listen through the city. Listen for the void. Listen for the nothing.

But there *is* no nothing.
All I hear is *him.*
Sound bites from his press conferences.
Spilling out of every screen in the city.
On the streets...people who love him, people who hate him...he's all they want to talk about.
And *I can hear every word.*
The city is *churning.* People are angry. They want answers. They want to be *safe*--and Fisk is promising them all of that and more.
It all feeds into his agenda. He wants the heroes *gone,* because he knows we'll fight him with everything we've got.
He needs to beat us, and he's using the strongest weapon he's got to do it.
WE *WILL NOT* LIVE IN--

FEAR.
GAH!

CHINATOWN.
DID YOU FIND MUSE?
I...NO. THERE'S...A LOT OF STATIC, BLINDSPO I CAN'T ZERO IN.

I'LL TRY AGAIN. GIVE ME A SECOND.
JUST NEED TO...PULL MYSELF TOGETHER.

YOU'VE ALREADY TRIED FOUR TIMES.
WHATEVER YOU DID WHEN YOU USED THAT TRICK TO FIND MUSE WHEN HE...WHEN HE HAD ME...IT DOESN'T SEEM TO WORK NOW.
I CAN GET IT.
OR MAYBE YOU'LL GET YOURSELF A STROKE.
DAMMIT!
KRRCK
FISK. IT'S FISK.
HE'S IN MY HEAD, SAM. I CAN'T GET HIM OUT. I CAN'T FOCUS.
BUT I HAVE A PLAN.
IN A FEW NIGHTS, HE'LL BE VULNERABLE. I'VE BEEN TALKING TO SOME OF THE OTHER HEROES, AND--

WAIT.
YOU'RE DEPUTY MAYOR.
IS THAT THE PLAN? YOU WANT TO TAKE HIM OUT SO YOU CAN BE MAYOR?
WHY DOES EVERYONE THINK... NO. THE ORDER OF SUCCESSION IN NEW YORK DOESN'T WORK THAT WAY. IT'S NOT LIKE VICE PRESIDENT.
IT'S...A COMPLICATED SITUATION. THERE'S A REASON FOR ALL OF IT.

TRUTH IS, IT DOESN'T MATTER TO ME WHO'S MAYOR. I DON'T REALLY LIVE IN THE SAME CITY YOU DO, YOU KNOW?
LOOK. THERE'S SOMETHING I NEED TO FINISH, BUT IF I CAN, I'LL HELP YOU, TOO.
WHAT DO YOU NEED TO...OH, NO, SAM. YOU CAN'T GO AFTER MUSE ALONE.
LISTEN-- REVENGE CAN FEEL LIKE THE ONLY THING THAT MATTERS, BUT I'VE BEEN DOWN THAT ROAD. IT'S *EMPTY.*
EVEN IF YOU GET WHAT YOU THINK YOU WANT, IT DOESN'T CHANGE ANYTHING. THE PAST IS STILL THE PAST.

UH, OKAY. NOTED. BUT YOU EVER THINK MAYBE I JUST DON'T WANT MUSE TO KILL ANYONE ELSE?
NEITHER DO I! I JUST THINK WE SHOULD TAKE HIM DOWN *TOGETHER.* JUST PROMISE ME...
WE TALKED ABOUT PROMISES, REMEMBER?
IF YOU DON'T MAKE THEM, YOU CAN'T BREAK THEM.
THANK YOU FOR TRYING. I'M SURE YOU DID EVERYTHING YOU COULD.

Did I?
Have I done *everything I can* to make sure Muse doesn't hurt anyone else?
No. I don't think I have.

CITY HALL.
Not yet.
MR. MURDOCK! WAIT!

YOU CAN'T JUST WALK IN THERE!
OH, I'M SORRY, I CAN'T HEAR YOU.

I THOUGHT YOU WERE BLIND, NOT DEAF.
WHO CAN REMEMBER?
I TOLD YOU, FISK.
I TOLD YOU PEOPLE WOULD DIE.
YOU SENT THE NYPD OUT AFTER MUSE, GUNS BLAZING, AND SIX OFFICERS DIED.
SO YOU DID. THE SOHO SIX. A TERRIBLE TRAGEDY.
FRANK CASTLE IS AN ANIMAL. I HOPE HE IS BROUGHT TO JUSTICE AS QUICKLY AS POSSIBLE.

YOU KNOW DAMN WELL THE PUNISHER DIDN'T KILL THEM. HE'D **NEVER** HURT A COP.
DO I KNOW THAT? DO I?
I THINK FRANK CASTLE WILL KILL ANYONE HE WANTS, IF HE THINKS IT'S WARRANTED. THAT'S THE PROBLEM--WITH HIM AND ALL THE VIGILANTES.
THEY BELIEVE THEY ARE A LAW UNTO THEMSELVES.

WHAT DO YOU WANT, MR. MURDOCK?
I WANT YOU TO STOP FOCUSING ON THE WRONG PROBLEM.
STOP DEMONIZING THE HEROES.
A SERIAL KILLER IS LOOSE IN YOUR CITY, AND I AM TELLING YOU--AGAIN--THAT THIS CITY'S ORDINARY LAW ENFORCEMENT IS NOT EQUIPPED TO HANDLE HIM.
SIX GOOD OFFICERS DIED TO PROVE ME RIGHT. IT DIDN'T HAVE TO HAPPEN.

TELL THE
LICE TO COORDINATE
ITH THE HEROES TO
ND MUSE AND BRING
HIM DOWN.
THEY HAVE THE SKILL, THE EXPERIENCE...THE *POWER.* LET THEM USE IT TO PROTECT YOUR CITY.

WHAT DO I WANT?
NO ONE ELSE TO DIE.
I SEE.

HERE IS WHAT I **NEED**, MR. MURDOCK.

I HAVE ARRANGED FOR A RALLY TO BE HELD THIS EVENING IN CENTRAL PARK. I KNOW THE CITY IS DIVIDED, AFRAID, CONFUSED. THIS EVENT IS INTENDED TO ADDRESS THAT PROBLEM.
YOU MAY NOT BELIEVE IT, BUT I DO HAVE NEW YORK'S BEST INTERESTS AT HEART.
I WANT YOU THERE, VISIBLE, AT MY SIDE, TANGIBLE EVIDENCE THAT MY ADMINISTRATION IS ABOUT COMPROMISE, ABOUT EMBRACING ALL VIEWPOINTS.
OR...
...YOU CAN QUIT.
IN WHICH CASE, YOU WOULD NEVER ENTER THIS OFFICE AGAIN. WHAT LITTLE INFLUENCE YOU HAVE ON MY POLICIES WOULD VANISH.
I WOULD THEN USE ALL MY POWER TO MAKE YOU A PARIAH IN THIS CITY. YOU WOULDN'T BE ABLE TO GET A JOB AS A FILE CLERK.

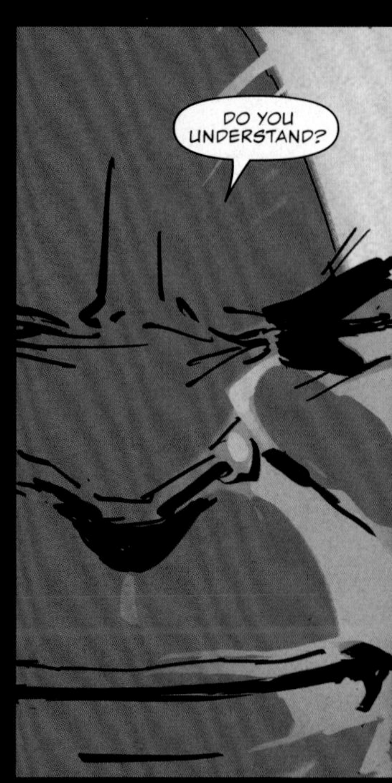
DO YOU UNDERSTAND?

SEEMS FAIRLY CLEAR, YES.

FINE. I'LL BE THERE. I'LL SMILE, WAVE, DO WHATEVER YOU WANT.
BUT JUST GIVE ME ONE THING.

DON'T DO ANYTHING TO PROVOKE MUSE, AT LEAST IN THE SHORT TERM.
PEOPLE ARE LOOKING FOR HIM-- IT'S POSSIBLE THAT THIS WHOLE PROBLEM COULD GO AWAY ON ITS OWN, WITHOUT YOU NEEDING TO KNOW ANYTHING ABOUT IT.
BUT MUSE IS COMPLETELY UNPREDICTABLE, AND CAPABLE OF TRULY HORRIBLE THINGS. JUST...DON'T FORCE HIS HAND. THAT'S ALL I'LL SAY.
I MAKE NO PROMISES.
I WILL HAVE THE DETAILS FOR TONIGHT'S EVENT SENT TO YOUR OFFICE. WE'RE DONE HERE.
FISK, YOU CAN'T JUST--
I AM THE MAYOR OF NEW YORK CITY. I WILL DO WHATEVER I THINK IS NECESSARY.
THAT IS MY JOB.
Yeah?
Not for long.

CHINATOWN.

CRKK

HA!
SAM! SAM! IT'S ME!

OH, HEY, HANNAH.
SORRY ABOUT THAT.
SORRY? SORRY? I HAVEN'T HEARD FROM YOU IN MONTHS, SAM!
I CAME UP HERE FOR A SMOKE, SAW A LIGHT ON IN HERE, AND...HOW ARE YOU HERE?
AND... YOUR EYES... AND MOM. IS MOM HERE?

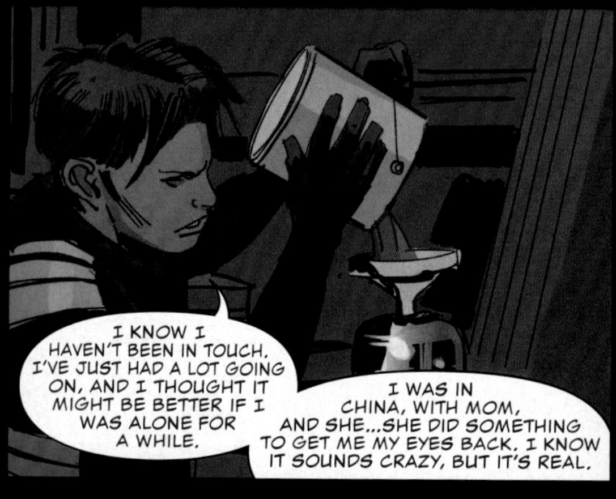
I KNOW I HAVEN'T BEEN IN TOUCH. I'VE JUST HAD A LOT GOING ON, AND I THOUGHT IT MIGHT BE BETTER IF I WAS ALONE FOR A WHILE.
I WAS IN CHINA, WITH MOM, AND SHE...SHE DID SOMETHING TO GET ME MY EYES BACK. I KNOW IT SOUNDS CRAZY, BUT IT'S REAL.

NOT SURE HOW I FEEL ABOUT THEM. THEY...THEY'RE STRANGE. THEY COST ME A LOT. BUT AT LEAST I CAN SEE.
AND MOM...
WHRR

...MOM'S STILL IN CHINA.

HNH, THERE WE GO.

SAM... ARE YOU ALL RIGHT?

I DON'T REALLY KNOW, HANNAH. T'S GETTING HARDER FOR ME TO TELL THE DIFFERENCE BETWEEN SOMETHING RIGHT AND SOMETHING WRONG.
WHEN YOU WORK ON THIS LEVEL, TRYING TO BE A SUPER HERO, LIFE AND DEATH...THERE'S ALL THESE *CONSEQUENCES.*
THINGS JUST *HAPPEN.*
I'M TRYING TO DO THINGS I **KNOW** ARE RIGHT WHEN I CAN. THAT'S ALL I CAN DO.
MUSE IS BACK. MAYBE YOU SAW THOSE PAINTINGS HE PUT UP ALL OVER THE CITY.
I'M GOING TO FIND HIM, AND MAKE SURE HE DOESN'T HURT ANYONE ELSE. I KNOW THAT'S RIGHT. I KNOW IT.

SAM... HE ***BLINDED*** YOU. HE'S A ***KILLER.***
I AM TOO, NOW. THAT'S SOMETHING ELSE I GOT IN CHINA. OR MAYBE SOMETHING I LOST. LIKE I SAID, IT'S HARD TO TELL.
AT LEAST... AT LEAST CALL ***DAREDEVIL.*** HE CAN ***HELP.***
NO, HE CAN'T. I'M DOING THIS ALONE. I NEED TO.

YOU'RE A GOOD PERSON. DON'T LET THIS CITY TAKE THAT AWAY FROM YOU.
WHY ARE YOU TALKING LIKE YOU'LL NEVER SEE ME AGAIN, SAM?

SAM?
I LOVE YOU, HANNAH.

BE GOOD.

I AM NOT A CROOK

WESLEY.
YES, SIR. HOW CAN I HELP?
I WANT THE MUSE MURALS GONE. ALL ACROSS THE CITY.
OF COURSE, SIR. RIGHT AWAY. AND IF I MAY, I'M GLAD YOU'VE FINALLY DECIDED TO DO THIS. I NEVER UNDERSTOOD WHY YOU LEFT THEM UP IN THE FIRST PLACE.

EVERY TIME ANYONE IN THIS CITY LOOKED AT THOSE MURALS, THEY THOUGHT OF SIX DEAD POLICE OFFICERS.
THEN THEY THOUGHT ABOUT THE COSTUMED VIGILANTE WHO KILLED THEM, AND THEY WONDERED IF THEY MIGHT BE NEXT.
AND THEN THEY THOUGHT ABOUT THEIR MAYOR'S PROMISE TO KEEP THEM SAFE.

BUT THEY'VE SERVED THEIR PURPOSE. THE SARNOS PROJECT IS ALMOST COMPLETE, AND I AM TIRED OF SEEING DAREDEVIL EVERY TIME I LOOK OUT MY WINDOW.
PAINT OVER THE MURALS. I REALIZE BOTH SARNOS AND THE RALLY IN CENTRAL PARK ARE LATER TONIGHT, BUT BEFORE THEN, IF POSSIBLE.
YES, SIR, OF COURSE. I'LL GET SANITATION ON IT RIGHT... AH...
HMM.
WESLEY?

MR. FISK... ARE YOU LOOKING OUT YOUR WINDOW RIGHT NOW?
NO. WHY?
WELL, SIR...

"...I THINK SOMEONE BEAT YOU TO IT."
FSSSH
FSSSSSHHHHHHH

OKAY, MUSE...
KLNG
...COME AND GET ME.

ALL RIGHT.
GAH!

I THINK FISK MAKES SOME REALLY GOOD POINTS, ACTUALLY...
FISK IS JUST GETTING STARTED--HE'S BEEN IN OFFICE FOR, WHAT, A MONTH? WE SHOULD JUST GIVE HIM A--
MAYOR WILSON FISK'S APPROVAL RATINGS ARE CLIMBING IN RESPONSE TO HIS HANDLING OF THE BRUTAL MURDER OF THE SOHO SIX--
AT THE MAYOR'S SURPRISE RALLY TONIGHT IN CENTRAL PARK, HE IS EXPECTED TO--
YOU REALLY THINK A CRIME BOSS SHOULD BE IN CHARGE OF--
I HOPE THEY CATCH THE PUNISHER SOON. FISK IS RIGHT--I'VE ALWAYS THOUGHT HE WAS A MANIAC.
MAYOR FISK GAVE A PRESS CONFERENCE AT--
EVER SINCE HE GOT ELECTED, I HAVEN'T BEEN SLEEPING WELL--
FISK ANNOUNCED AN INITIATIVE TO BETTER POLICE--
ME GUSTA EL ALCALDE FISK--
I RESPECT THAT FISK BROUGHT THAT MURDOCK GUY ON BOARD.
SAY WHAT YOU WANT--FISK AIN'T BACKING DOWN FROM NOBODY.
FISK
FISK
FISK SAID
MAYOR FISK
FISK APPEARED
FISK
FISK
MAYOR FISK
FISK
ALCALDE FISK
MAIRE FISK DISAIT
Enough.
THANK YOU. ALL OF YOU.
I'M GLAD YOU'RE HERE.

LET ME TELL YOU HOW WE'LL TAKE DOWN THE KINGPIN.

600

The Kingpin has already lost.
He just doesn't realize it yet. New York is my city. Not his.
No.
I'm wrong.
It's ours.
Spider-Man.
Moon Knight.
Misty Knight.
Echo.
Iron Fist.
Luke Cage.
Jessica Jones.
Daredevil.
We protect this city, we fight in its streets, we are New York.
And now we'll take it back from Wilson Fisk.
Mayor or not, he has to go down. We agree on that.

'S KITCHEN.
LIER.
YOU THINK WE CAN JUST... TAKE DOWN THE MAYOR? JUST LIKE THAT?
YOU'RE INSANE.
WE GONNA IMPEACH HIM OR SOMETHING?
MAYORS DON'T GET IMPEACHED, LUKE--NOT WITHOUT CAUSE. AND EVEN THEN, THE GOVERNOR HAS TO STEP IN.
THERE'S A CHANCE HE'D DO THAT, BUT ONLY IF WE GIVE HIM A GOOD REASON.
I THINK WE CAN.
MATT MURDOCK PASSED ME INFORMATION ABOUT A MEET TONIGHT.
BEFORE FISK HOLDS HIS RALLY IN CENTRAL PARK, HE'LL BE WITH CRIME BOSSES FROM ALL OVER THE CITY UP IN THE BRONX.
THE OWL, HAMMERHEAD, MORE.
HE'S GOING TO GIVE THEM MAYORAL APPOINTMENTS-- CARVE UP NEW YORK LIKE A--
LET ME.
LET YOU WHAT?
LET ME SAY IT.
UH...
I'M JUST GONNA SAY IT.
THE KINGPIN'S GONNA CARVE UP NEW YORK LIKE A BIG APPLE PIE.
BIG.
APPLE.
BECAUSE NEW YORK IS THE...
EH. WHATEVER.

PROCEED.

HEAR THE
IN MAKING
DEALS.
THEN, THANKS TO THE SLUGANSKY RULING, I CAN TESTIFY IN COURT, OR EVEN GO STRAIGHT TO THE GOVERNOR.
THIS IS LIKE WHEN WE HELPED YOU WITH AMMO AND THE CLIP.
EXACTLY, ECHO. JUST LIKE THAT--BUT ON A LARGER SCALE.
SO...IT'S JUST A STAKEOUT? I GET IT--DO IT ALL THE TIME--BUT WHY DO YOU NEED US?
INSURANCE, MISTY. ONCE I HEAR WHAT I NEED, I'LL CALL IN THE COPS TO ARREST EVERYONE--BUT THAT COULD TAKE TIME.
YOUR JOB WILL BE TO MAKE SURE NO ONE LEAV BEFORE WE CAN G FISK AND THE OTHE IN CUFFS.
LISTEN--I'M JUST GONNA SAY THIS. WHAT MAKES YOU THINK THE COPS WILL DO ANYTHING AT ALL? WON'T THEY JUST ARREST *US?*
I'M WITH JESS. YOU'RE PUBLIC ENEMY NUMBER ONE, DAREDEVIL, AND THE REST OF US AREN'T MUCH BETTER. NOT IN *FISK'S* NEW YORK.
I KNOW YOU THINK MURDOCK'S A GENIUS, BUT ARE YOU *ABSOLUTELY CERTAIN* THIS PLAN IS SOLID?
MURDOCK KNOWS WHAT HE'S DOING. AS FOR THE COPS...THEY DON'T WANT THE KINGPIN IN OFFICE ANY MORE THAN WE DO.
THEY JUST A NEED A *REASON TO ACT.* WE'LL GIVE IT TO THEM. THEY'LL MAKE THE RIGHT CHOICE.
THIS IS THE MOMENT. THIS IS WHEN IT HAPPENS. I KNOW IT.
NOW.
Sarno's
RESTAURANT
I *know it.*
The others do too, no matter what they say. That's why they came.
No Blindspot, though. He said he'd be here if he could. I believe that. He wants to help, even after everything that's happened to him.
I hope he's all right. Blindspot's *young.* Youth means mistakes. It's the way of things. You learn, you move on.
But in the super hero world...

there's no
m for error.
DOWNTOW
NO!
THIS IS WHAT YOU WANTED, BLINDSPOT. OTHERWISE YOU'D NEVER HAVE COME DOWN HERE AND DESTROYED ONE OF MY MURALS.
THIS IS EXACTLY WHAT YOU WANTED.

YOU HAD TO KNOW I'D RESPOND LIKE THIS.

YOU HAD TO SEE THE FORESHADOWING.

THIS IS THE STORY YOU WANTED ME TO TELL.
WHP
AAGH!

AH. YOU'RE STILL ALIVE. I REALLY THOUGHT YOU WERE DEAD JUST THERE.
I SUPPOSE WE CAN CALL THIS THE LATEST EXCITING TWIST IN THE SAGA OF MUSE AND BLINDSPOT, EH?

I'VE GOT ANOTHER ONE FOR YOU.
IMAGINE THE TENSION IF WE PUT OFF THE FINAL BATTLE FOR ANOTHER DAY.
YOU DEFACED MY WORK...BUT I'M WILLING TO LET THAT GO, JUST FOR TONIGHT, IN SERVICE OF THE GREATER STORY.
BLINDSPOT VS. MUSE... ONE FOR THE AGES!
WHY NOT KEEP THEM WAITING? TENSION CAN BE A POWERFUL ARTISTIC TOOL.

NO? YOU'D RATHER CLIMB UP HERE AND HASH THIS OUT NOW?
NNNGH

I CAN MAKE THAT WORK.

THE BRONX. SARNO'S.
HELLO, FELICIA. FASHIONABLY LATE, I SEE.
I DO EVERYTHING FASHIONABLY, LELAND.
BESIDES YOU, I SEE DIAMONDBACK AND HAMMERHEAD.
A MAN WHO TRIED TO KILL ME, AND A MAN WHO, LAST I CHECKED, WORKS FOR ME.
BUT I DON'T SEE THE KINGPIN.

FISK'S THE MAYOR OF NEW YORK CITY. HE SHOWS UP WHENEVER THE HELL HE WANTS.
MAYBE HE HAS STUFF TO DO FOR THAT RALLY HE'S THROWIN' IN THE PARK LATER.
FOR WHAT HE'S GONNA GIVE US, I'M WILLING TO WAIT.
THAT'S THE BEAUTY OF THIS, FELICIA. FISK CHANGED THE GAME. ALL THE OLD GRUDGES, THE TURF BATTLES...THEY DON'T MATTER ANYMORE.
FOR ONCE... WE'RE ALL ON THE SAME TEAM.
YEAH, OWLSLEY'S RIGHT, SEE? NEW YORK'S A BIG TOWN. PLENTY TO GO AROUND.

PLENTY FOR ALL OF US.
HNH.
I'VE BEEN THINKING ABOUT THIS PLAN, DAREDEVIL. IT SEEMS SOMEWHAT... INVOLVED. I HAVE ANOTHER IDEA.

WE ALL GO IN TOGETHER AND BEAT THEM HALF TO DEATH.
MOON KNIGHT...NO. IF WE DO THIS RIGHT, WE GET THE WHOLE HOUSE OF CARDS.
UNTIL FISK GETS HERE, WE HAVE NOTHING.

"WE WAIT."

DOWNTOWN.
CAN I ASK YOU SOMETHING, BLINDSPOT?
DIDN'T I PULL OUT YOUR EYES NOT SO LONG AGO?
YOU WOULDN'T BE ABLE TO FIGHT LIKE THIS IF YOU WERE BLIND, THOUGH. YOU MUST HAVE FOUND NEW EYES SOMEWHERE.
GOOD FOR YOU.
MAKES ME WONDER WHY YOU'RE SO ANGRY, THOUGH.
AFTER ALL, YOU FIXED YOUR EYES...
WHP
...WHO'S GOING TO FIX MY ART?
DON'T YOU REALIZE I PUT THOSE MURALS UP TO HELP PEOPLE LIKE YOU?
AGH!
KRRK

HELICOPTERS.
WAS...
...INSPIRING.
BEAUTIFUL, SHARED DELUSION. I LOVE IT.
I WISH YOU COULD JUST GET WITH THE PROGRAM, BUT OBVIOUSLY THAT'S NEVER GOING TO HAPPEN.
MAKES ME THINK I SHOULD TAKE YOUR EYES AGAIN, BUT THAT WOULD BE REPEATING MYSELF--STEALING FROM MY OWN INSPIRATION.
I NEED SOMETHING FRESH.
YOUR TONGUE, MAYBE? HM.
BLINDSPOT.
SAMUEL

YES.
YOU HEAR ME, OATHBREAKER.
DO YOU WANT TO LIVE SAMUEL? TO DEFEAT THIS.. MUSE?
YOU KNOW MY POWER. THE POWER OF THE BEAST. I WILL GIVE IT TO YOU ONCE AGAIN.
JUST REAC OUT..
...AND TAKE IT.

FWSSH
MUSE!
ENOUGH!
THWM
YOU'VE... CHANGED, BLINDSPOT.
TH-THAT'S GOOD. CHANGE IS GOOD.
CHANGE IS HOW WE GR--
SHUT UP.
KRCK

FISK IS LATE. SIGNIFICANTLY LATE. THIS ISN'T LIKE HIM.
STARTIN' TO WONDER ABOUT THIS MYSELF. SMELLIN' LIKE A SETUP.
YOU KNOW WHAT I THINK?
FISK WANTS US TO KILL EACH OTHER.
OF US COULD MAKE REAL TROUBLE FOR HIM IN HIS NEW GIG. WE KNOW WHO HE REALLY IS. WE KNOW WHERE HE'S BURIED THE BODIES.
MUCH MORE CONVENIENT FOR HIM IF WE TAKE EACH OTHER OUT. SO HE PROMISES US WHATEVER WILL GET US IN A ROOM TOGETHER, AND THEN...LETS NATURE TAKE ITS COURSE.
MAYBE YOU'RE RIGHT, KITTY CAT. BUT IF IT REALLY IS INEVITABLE, THEN I SAY...
DON'T LIKE THE BODY LANGUAGE IN THERE, MISTY.
YEAH, ECHO, I KNOW. THAT ROOM IS LOOKING TENSE.

...WHY WAIT?

THWIPP
WHAT THE--

RAT-A-TAT-ATT
HOW 'BOUT YOU EAT LEAD, SPIDER-MAN!
HEY HEY!
WHAT IF WE SKIP THE WHOLE GANGLAND SHOOT-'EM-UP THING?
MAYBE WE ALL GET SOME CANNOLI? I BET THIS PLACE HAS GREAT CANNOLI, AND HONESTLY, I'M STARV--

HUH. THAT WAS ACTUALLY... PRETTY GOOD, HAMMERHEAD.

NOW, LOOK. I REALIZE YOU ALL BROUGHT A LOT OF GUNS, AND IT'S SORT OF A WASTE NOT TO SHOOT THEM.
BUT IF YOU REALLY HAVE TO SHOOT AT SOMEONE...

...MAYBE JUST AIM AT MY FRIEND OVER THERE.

I'M BULLETPROOF.
UH, HONEY... YOU DO KNOW I'M STANDING RIGHT NEXT TO YOU?
KILL THESE &%@&S!
WHAT...WHAT IS HAPPENING?
KRSH
VENGEANCE!
SO... I GUESS WE'RE GOING IN?
SEEMS THAT WAY. NO SURPRISE THERE. YOU SURPRISED?
NOPE. SAW THIS COMING A MILE AWAY.
I'M DEAF, NO BLIND.

Damn. Damn.
So much for the plan.
Need to get down there, before someone gets--
Wait.
NYPD. But that's...
Oh, no.
SPIDER-MAN! LUKE! YOU'VE GOT SQUADS OF NYPD PX UNITS MOVING TOWARD THE BUILDING FROM ALL SIDES!
YOU ALREADY CALLED THE COPS? MAN, THEY GOT HERE FAST.
MAYBE IT'S FOR THE BEST. THIS IS GETTING PRETTY--
LUKE, NO.
I DIDN'T CALL ANYONE YET.
WELL, CRUD.

THIS WHOLE THING WAS A SETUP. A TRAP.
LOOKS THAT WAY, DAREDEVIL, BUT WE CAN'T RUN.
IF WE LEAVE, THESE IDIOTS WILL KILL EACH OTHER--OR THEY'LL KILL THE COPS.

I KNOW. I'M COMING. WE'LL DO WHAT WE CAN.
NO. DON'T.
YOU HAVE TO GET TO YOUR FRIEND MURDOCK. HE WORKS WITH FISK.

MURDOCK'S OUR ONLY SHOT.
ALL... ALL RIGHT. I'LL TRY.

PFSSH
ALL OF YOU...LISTEN TO ME. I PROMISE YOU.

I WILL FIX THIS.

DOWNTOWN.
I NEED TO UNDERSTAND, MUSE.
I NEED THIS TO MAKE SENSE.
WHY DO YOU DO WHAT YOU DO?
WHY DO YOU HURT PEOPLE? WHY DO YOU KILL?
WHY?
YOU KNOW WHY, BLINDSPOT.
IT'S THE SAME REASON YOU WANT TO KILL ME RIGHT NOW.
IT MAKES YOU STRONG
IT MAKES YOU BETTER
IT SHOWS THEM YOUR POWER
IT SAYS SOMETHING
IT MEANS SOMETHING
IT SOLVES YOUR PROBLEMS
IT GIVES YOU CONTROL
YOU'RE BIG
THEY'RE SMALL
IT'S ART
IT'S ART
IT'S ART!

IT'S ART! IT'S ART!
SHUT UP!
I'LL KILL YOU IF YOU DON'T SHUT UP!
DO IT.
YOU HAVE TAKEN OUR GIFTS, SAMUEL...NOW, YOU MUST REPAY US.
ONE DEATH. A SMALL THING.
THINK OF HOW MANY LIVES MUSE'S DEATH WILL SAVE.
THIS IS A SMALL THING WE ASK.
NO...NO...
YOU WANT THIS. YOU KNOW HE WILL KILL YOU IF YOU DO NOT KILL HIM. YOU DO NOT WANT TO TRADE YOUR LIFE FOR HIS.
REJECT US, AND WE WILL COME FOR YOU. YOU CANNOT USE OUR POWER AND NOT EXPECT TO PAY.
NO. I DO REJECT YOU.
I REJECT DEATH.
GAH!
KRCK

NO. I DON'T LIKE THIS.
I'M THE STORY.
I'M THE STORY.

I'M THE SONG.
NOT YOU, BLINDSPOT.
NOT YOU.

I WON'T ALLOW IT.

I... HAD SO MUCH...

...BEAUTY LEFT.
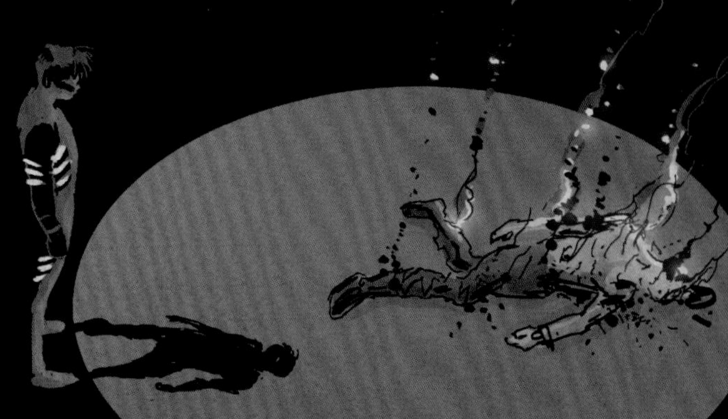

HOW MANY ARE OUT THERE, WESLEY?
THE RALLY WASN'T TICKETED, SO IT'S HARD TO SAY FOR SURE, MR. FISK. THE PARKS DEPARTMENT'S ESTIMATING ABOUT 200,000.
GOOD. AND THE OTHER THING?
THE POLICE COMMISSIONER JUST CHECKED IN. SUCCESSFUL RAID. THEY GOT THEM ALL.
ALL FOUR?
FISK
FISK
FISK
FISK
CENTRAL PARK. THE GREAT LAWN.
BELVEDERE CASTLE.
YES--AND A GOOD NUMBER OF THEIR SOLDIERS, TOO. THEY STARTED SOME SORT OF GUN BATTLE. PLENTY OF EVIDENCE TO PUT THEM ALL AWAY.
IDIOTS.
ALL RIGHT. THAT WILL GIVE ME THE BOOST I'M LOOKING FOR. WE WON'T NEED MURDOCK ANYMORE.
YOU WANT ME TO TELL HIM HE'S OUT RIGHT NOW? I'M NOT SURE HE'S HERE YET, BUT...
MM...NO. LET HIM STAND NEXT TO ME ON THAT STAGE, OBLIVIOUS TO WHAT'S COMING. I'LL USE HIM TONIGHT, FIRE HIM ON MONDAY. I'D LIKE TO DO IT TO HIS FACE.
EXCELLENT, MR. FISK. I LIKE IT. AND I HAVE MORE GOOD NEWS, TOO.
YOU'RE SMILING, WESLEY. WHAT IS IT?
THE NYPD DIDN'T JUST GET THE CRIME BOSSES, SIR.

THERE WERE HEROES THERE, TOO.
JESSICA JONES, DANNY RAND, MAYA LOPEZ, LUKE CAGE, MISTY KNIGHT AND MARC SPECTOR.
EVEN SPIDER-MAN.
SPIDER-MAN...
AND WHAT IS HIS NAME? WHO IS HE?
WE DON'T KNOW. JUST BEFORE THE COPS GRABBED HIM, HE SPRAYED THAT WEBBING OF HIS AROUND HIS NECK. SEALED IT UP TIGHT, LIKE GLUE.
THEY CAN'T GET HIS MASK OFF.
HNH. TYPICAL.
WELL, THAT WEBBING DOESN'T LAST FOREVER. OR WE'LL CUT HIS MASK OFF, IF WE HAVE TO.
PLEASE OFFER MY CONGRATULATIONS TO COMMISSIONER KARNIK. EXCELLENT WORK. BUT I NEED TO ASK...
I KNOW, SIR. DAREDEVIL.
HE WASN'T WITH THE GROUP. WE DON'T KNOW WHERE HE--
THMP
YOU DON'T THINK...
ACTUALLY, I DO.
IT'D BE JUST LIKE HIM.
COME ALONG, WESLEY.
LET'S GO UP AND SAY HELLO.

FISK.
I CAN GET THE COPS, SIR. WE'VE GOT OFFICERS ALL OVER DOWN THERE.
NO, WESLEY. GO BACK DOWNSTAIRS, WAIT FOR MY CALL.
DAREDEVIL AND I ARE GOING TO HAVE A LITTLE TALK.
NOW, WHAT CAN I DO FOR YOU?
YOU CAN ORDER THE RELEASE OF THE HEROES THE NYPD JUST TOOK INTO CUSTODY.
THEY WERE THERE TO SAVE LIVES. THAT'S ALL.
YOU'LL LET THEM GO. RIGHT NOW.

OR WHAT?

YOU WERE THERE, I'M GUESSING.
EAVESDROPPING LIKE SOME PERVERT, LOOKING FOR SOMETHING TO USE AGAINST ME.
BUT ALL YOU FOUND WAS A MAYOR EXECUTING A PLAN TO KEEP HIS CITY SAFE FROM...
...CRIMINAL ELEMENTS.
IF MY NAME WEREN'T WILSON FISK, YOU WOULDN'T HAVE BATTED AN EYE.
YOU'D BE CHEERING THAT THE MAYOR HAD FOUND A WAY TO GET OWLSLEY AND THE OTHERS OFF THE STREETS.
BUT YOU ARE WILSON FISK. YOU ARE THE KINGPIN.
AND YOU'RE THE ENEMY OF EVERYTHING THAT MATTERS ABOUT THIS CITY.
NO, I'M NOT.
I hear the rasp of his hands tightening on the hammer.
An intake of breath.
BUT I'M SICK OF TRYING TO EXPLAIN THAT TO YOU.
WSSH
It was always going to end this way.

YOU WANT ME TO HIT YOU, WILSON. I WON'T DO IT. I WON'T GIVE YOU MORE AMMUNITION AGAINST ME, MORE BRUISES YOU CAN POINT TO, CAUSED BY THE EVIL VIGILANTE.
BUT MY FISTS AREN'T MY ONLY WEAPONS.

YOU HAVE NO IDEA WHAT I'M CAPABLE OF. THE ONLY THING THAT'S EVER HELD ME BACK IS THE LAW.
GRAH!
KRRNCH

YOU TAKE THAT AWAY FROM ME...YOU TAKE AWAY MY LIMITS.
YOU'LL SEE WHAT THAT...
ENOUGH. PLEASE. ENOUGH OF YOUR SILLY, ENDLESS SPEECHES.

YOU POOR IDIOT...DON'T YOU SEE YOU'VE ALREADY LOST?
WE'RE NOT EVEN PLAYING THE SAME GAME ANYMORE. I RUN A CITY OF EIGHT MILLION PEOPLE.
YOU'RE JUST SO...

...SMALL-TIME.

I LOVE THIS CITY. I ALWAYS HAVE.
I THINK OF ALL THE TIME I WASTED ON YOU, ON PEOPLE LIKE YOU... IT MAKES ME SICK.
ALL ALONG, I SHOULD HAVE BEEN GOING AFTER THIS.
ALL THIS POWER...AS THE MAYOR...I CAN DO ANYTHING I WANT.
AND WHAT I WANT...IS TO FIX NEW YORK.
What is he doing? With the hammer... he's going to...
YOU WON'T STOP ME.
NO ONE WILL.
No...not again. Wesley saw me up here--Fisk can blame whatever he does to himself on me, make things even worse...
SORRY, FISK.
NOT THIS TIME. NO MORE FALSE ASSAULT CLAIMS. WHEN I BEAT YOU, IT WON'T BE THIS WAY.
I WON'T LAY A FINGER ON YOU.
WHP
TRUE.

THWM
NNGH!
THD
THE ONLY HERO THIS CITY NEEDS...
KRCK
...IS ITS KING.

I...
...LOVE...

FnIySck
...NEW YORK!

LOOK AT THAT. THEY'RE EATING IT UP.
WELL, WHY WOULDN'T THEY? HE **DOES** LOVE NEW YORK, RIGHT, MR. WESLEY?
MORE THAN ANYONE I'VE EVER MET, STEVE.

WE'RE HERE TONIGHT TO CELEBRATE THIS WONDERFUL CITY...TO REMIND OURSELVES THAT WHEN NEW YORKERS COME TOGETHER, THERE IS **NOTHING** WE CAN'T ACCOMPLISH.
THANK YOU FOR THE TRUST YOU'VE PUT IN ME AS YOUR MAYOR-- KNOW THAT I DON'T TAKE IT FOR GRANTED.
I WILL CONTINUE TO **EARN** THAT TRUST BY WORKING **TIRELESSLY** FOR THIS CITY.
FnIySck

IN FACT, JUST TONIGHT I GOT WORD FROM THE POLICE COMMISSIONER THAT A **STING** OPERATION WE'VE BEEN PLANNING SINCE I TOOK OFFICE WAS SUCCESSFULLY CONCLUDED.
FOUR MAJOR CITY CRIME BOSSES, AS WELL AS A NUMBER OF COSTUMED VIGILANTES, WERE APPREHENDED AND ARE NOW IN CUSTODY.
NEW YORK CITY IS SAFER THAN--

WHSSS-THK
NNH?

W-WHAT?

SSSK
FTHK
FTHK
AGH!
FTHK
FTHK
FTHK
FTHK
NNNNGH

NINJAS? WHAT THE HELL ARE YOU TALKING ABOUT? OVER.
NINJAS! HUNDREDS, MAYBE THOUSANDS! THEY'RE ALL AROUND THE PARK, AND WE'VE GOT REPORTS THEY'RE POPPING UP ALL ACROSS THE CITY. PEOPLE ARE PANICKING.
THEY ATTACKED MAYOR FISK...SHOT HIM FULL OF ARROWS. WE NEED ALL PX UNITS UP AT THE CASTLE TO MAKE SURE WE CAN GET HIM OUT SAFELY.
Ninjas...the Hand. And they've come in force.
But...Fisk? Why would they go after Fisk?
ROGER THAT. WE NEED TO SECURE OUR PRISONER, THEN WE'LL BE THERE. HOLD TIGHT.
LISTEN TO ME. I KNOW WHAT THIS IS. I'VE FOUGHT THESE THINGS BEFORE.
THEY'RE DEADLY, AND THEY AREN'T EXACTLY ALIVE. THEY DON'T FEEL PAIN, AND CAN TAKE ENORMOUS DAMAGE. YOU HAVE TO GO FOR THE KILL SHOT, EVERY TIME. NO WARNINGS, NO--
YEAH, THANKS.
No. This can't be about the Kingpin. This is about me. And Blindspot.
The Beast is here to take back what it's owed.
YOU NEED TO LET ME OUT OF THESE CUFFS. I CAN HELP. PEOPLE WILL DIE.
NOT GONNA HAPPEN.

JUST LET ME HELP.
The Beast knows me. It knows I defend this city. It knows I love New York.
So it took it away.
LET'S GO.
POLICE

Back's in agony--can barely *think* after those cheap shots from Fisk.
Set that aside, Matt. Reach out...listen... find out what's happening.

ALL RIGHT, THE MAYOR IS OUT OF COMMISSION. ORDER OF SUCCESSION'S IN EFFECT. WE NEED THE PUBLIC ADVOCATE TO ASSUME CONTROL.
I'VE ALREADY CONTACTED HER, COMMISSIONER. SHE'S HEADED TO CITY HALL NOW.
UH...EXCUSE ME, BUT THAT'S NOT RIGHT.

WHAT? WHO THE HELL ARE YOU?
MY NAME'S STEVE CORNISH. I WORK IN THE MAYOR'S OFFICE.
I KNOW THE ORDER OF SUCCESSION NORMALLY SAYS THE PUBLIC ADVOCATE TAKES OVER IF THE MAYOR'S INCAPACITATED.
BUT MAYOR FISK HAD ME READING OVER ALL THE OLD RULES AND REGULATIONS FROM PRIOR ADMINISTRATIONS, AND THE LAST GUY...HE *CHANGED* IT.

IT WAS WHEN HE ADJUSTED THINGS TO LET HIMSELF HAVE A THIRD TERM.
MAYBE FISK WOULD HAVE CHANGED IT BACK EVENTUALLY... BUT HE *DIDN'T.* HASN'T HAD TIME, I GUESS. SO, THAT NEW RULE IS STILL IN EFFECT.

THE DEPUTY MAYOR KNOWS ALL THIS, ACTUALLY. I WENT OVER ALL OF IT WITH HIM. READ HIM EVERY LAST WORD.
THE *DEPUTY MAYOR?* WAIT, SO THAT MEANS...
OH NO, NO, NO...

YUP.

MATT MURDOCK IS THE MAYOR OF NEW YORK CITY.
TO BE CONTINUED...

HELL'S KITCHEN.
I'M GOING AFTER THE OTHER MUGGERS.
GET HIM TO A HOSPITAL. TWO CRACKED RIBS, LIKELY CONCUSSION.
GOT IT.
HEY! POLICE! THIS GUY JUST GOT MUGGED!
DAMN, DUDE...
Manganaro
488
GROSSERIA
...YOU KNOW DAREDEVIL? THAT IS DOPE!
HUH? OH...
...NO, HE JUST TOLD ME TO GET THIS GUY HELP, THAT'S ALL.
YEAH, BUT HE TALKED TO YOU LIKE HE KNOWS YOU, MAN. LIKE HE TRUSTS YOU TO TAKE CARE OF BUSINESS, KNOW WHAT I'M SAYIN'?
GRO
WHO ARE YOU, ANYWAY?

COLUMBIA UNIVERSITY.
YEARS AGO.
THIS IS GONNA BE SO GREAT!
YOU HAVE NO IDEA HOW LUCKY YOU ARE, MURDOCK, 'CAUSE FOGGY NELSON JUST HAPPENS TO BE THE FINEST WINGMAN IN THE HISTORY OF WINGMEN.

YOU JUST STAND THERE LOOKING HANDSOME, STRONG, STOIC...WITH A HINT OF TRAGEDY, WHILE I DRAW 'EM IN WITH MY ORATORICAL VIRTUOSITY.
BETWEEN MY SILVER TONGUE, YOUR LOOKS, AND THE WHOLE BLIND THING, YOU'RE GONNA NEED THAT CANE TO WARD OFF THE BABES!

OH... OH, MAN. MATT, I AM SO SORRY. SOMETIMES MY MOUTH GETS AHEAD OF MY BRAIN.
IF I OFFENDED YOU--

I'M ONLY OFFENDED WHEN PEOPLE PITY ME.
SINCE I SET FOOT ON CAMPUS, YOU'RE THE ONLY ONE WHO HASN'T.
NOW TELL ME MORE ABOUT THE GAME PLAN, COACH.

OKAY, SO WHEN YOU'VE TALKED WITH A GIRL A WHILE AND YOU'RE HITTING IT OFF, DO THE WHOLE SHY, TENTATIVE "CAN I TOUCH YOUR FACE" BIT. THAT'S GOLD!
AW, THIS IS GONNA BE EPIC...

IS IT GREAT, OR IS IT THE GREATEST?
EQUAL PARTNERS, OF COURSE. IT JUST HAS A BETTER RING TO IT WITH MY NAME FIRST, DON'TCHA THINK?
THIS TOWN'S NEVER SEEN LAWYERS LIKE US!
NELSON AND MURDOCK
ATTORNEYS AT LAW

MY PARTNER SENDS HIS DEEPEST REGRETS THAT HE COULDN'T BE HERE. HE...HAD A MINOR ACCIDENT.
I DON'T KNOW IF YOU'VE HEARD, BUT HE'S BLIND, THE POOR GUY...

YOUR HONOR, IF WE COULD HAVE JUST A FEW MORE MINUTES?
I KNOW MY CO-COUNSEL IS ON HIS WAY, AND HE'S THE ONE WHO PREPARED THE OPENING STATEMENT...

OKAY, I'LL GIVE THE OPENING STATEMENT.
NOT LIKE I'VE NEVER HAD TO WING IT BEFORE...

BAR
JOSIE'S
GRILL
HEY, JOSIE, I HEARD... Y'KNOW, AROUND THE NEIGHBORHOOD... YOU'RE HAVING PROBLEMS GETTING THE INSURANCE COMPANY TO FIX THE WINDOW.
NELSON & MURDOCK CAN HELP, PRO BONO.
THAT BETTER MEAN "FREE."
MATT? GOOD NEWS. I FOUND CASE LAW THAT APPLIES TO THE BRUCE BANNER TRIAL...
YOUR HONOR, MATTHEW MURDOCK CONTINUES TO FIGHT THE BRIBERY CHARGES AGAINST HIM, WHICH HE VEHEMENTLY DENIES.
HE HAS ALREADY BEEN DISBARRED, AND I WOULD REMIND THE COURT HE IS BLIND... NOT A FLIGHT RISK OR A DANGER TO ANYONE.
PRISON, AT THIS POINT, WOULD BE BOTH UNNECESSARY AND UNJUST.

WE DID IT, BUDDY. YOU'RE A LAWYER AGAIN!

I PRONOUNCE THIS COUPLE TO BE HUSBAND AND WIFE.

THE DOCTOR SAID THE DRUG MR. FEAR DOSED MILLA WITH MIGHT'VE DONE...UM, PERMANENT DAMAGE.
BUT WE'RE GONNA DO EVERYTHING WE CAN, MATT...SHE'LL HAVE THE BEST POSSIBLE CARE, I'LL MAKE SURE OF THAT.

AW, MATT...NOT AGAIN...
I NEED HELP HERE!
MY FRIEND, HE...HE GOT MUGGED.
THANKS FOR YOUR DISCRETION, NURSE... UH...
NURSE NURSE.
JUST "NIGHT NURSE."

LOOKS GREAT.
YOU'RE BLIND.

WHEN YOU PUT ON THAT MASK AND GO OUT THERE AND DO STUPID &$%# LIKE THIS--IT PUTS US ALL AT RISK, MATT!

I'M NOT DARE DEVIL

SNNRXXXX...

ME?
I'M JUST A GUY, KID.
NOBODY SPECIAL.
THEY ALSO SERVE

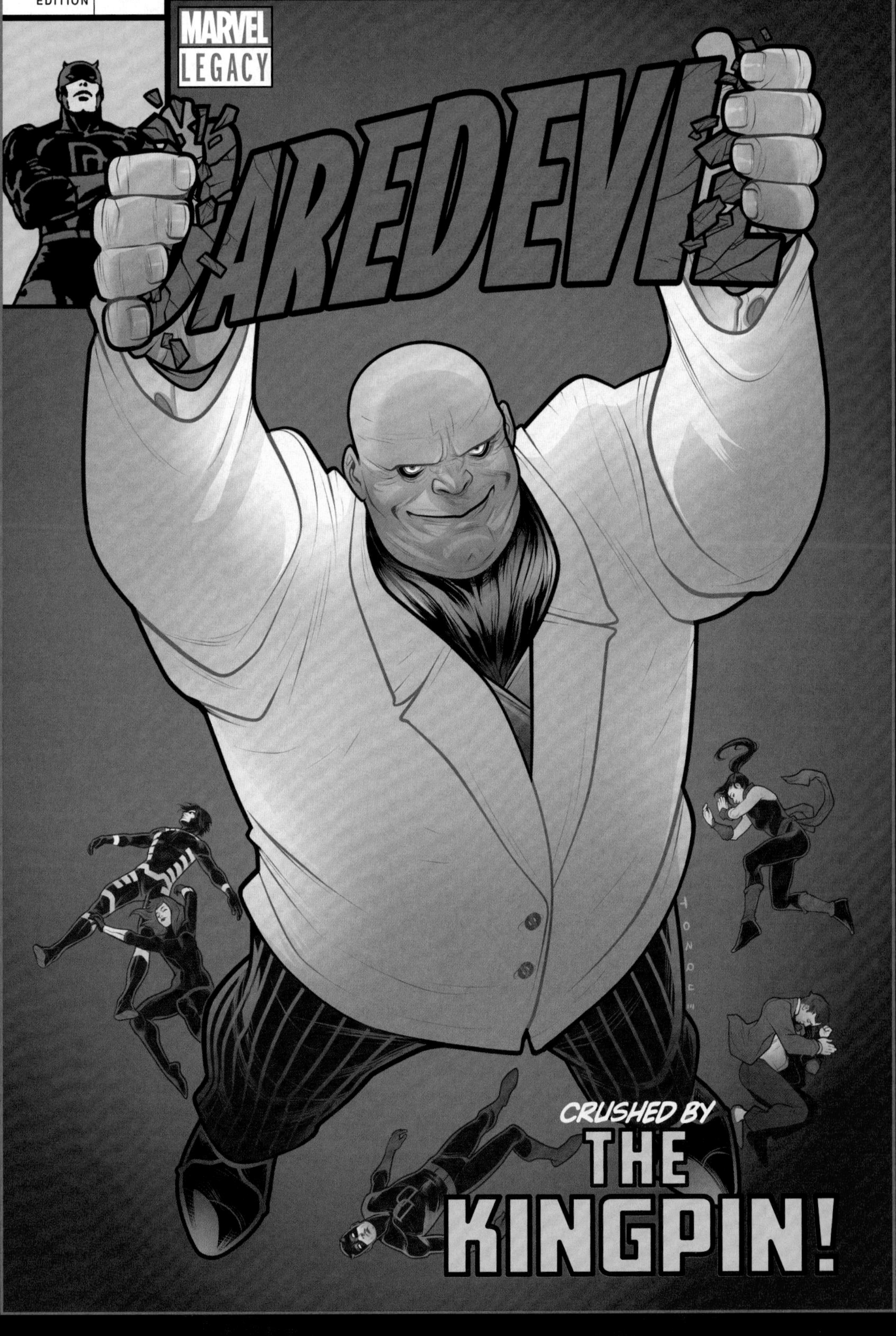

ELIZABETH TORQUE
No. 595 LEGACY VARIANT

DECLAN SHALVEY & JORDIE BELLAIRE

No. 595 VARIANT

JACK KIRBY
No. 595 1965 T-SHIRT VARIANT

MIKE McKONE & RACHELLE ROSENBERG
No. 595 LEGACY HEADSHOT VARIANT

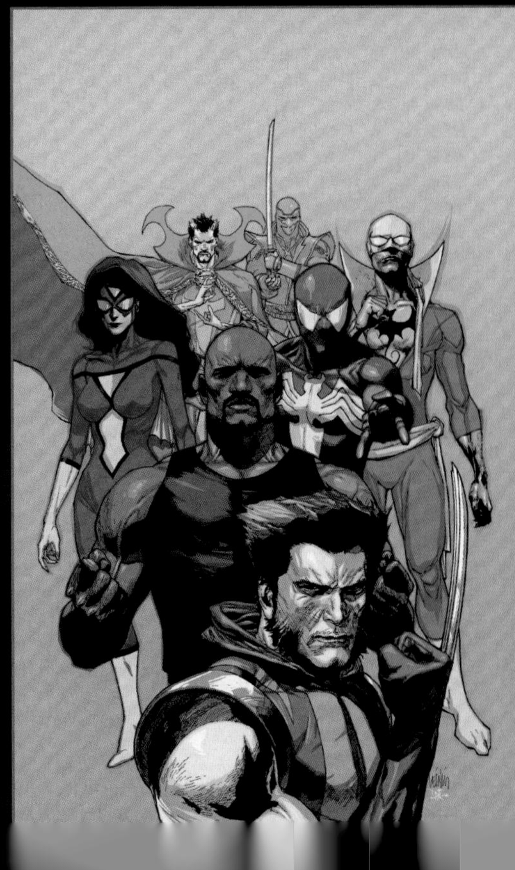

JOE QUESADA &
RICHARD ISANOVE
No. 600 VARIANT

JOE QUESADA
& RICHARD ISANOVE
No. 600 VARIANT

ADI GRANOV
No. 600 VARIANT

ADI GRANOV

No. 600 VARIANT

FRANK MILLER WITH **JOE FRONTIRRE**
No. 600 REMASTERED BLACK AND WHITE VARIANT

FRANK MILLER WITH **DEAN WHITE & JOE FRONTIRRE**
No. 600 REMASTERED VARIANT

JOHN ROMITA & CHRIS SOTOMAYOR
No. 600 VARIANT

JOHN TYLER CHRISTOPHER
No. 600 TRADING CARD VARIANT

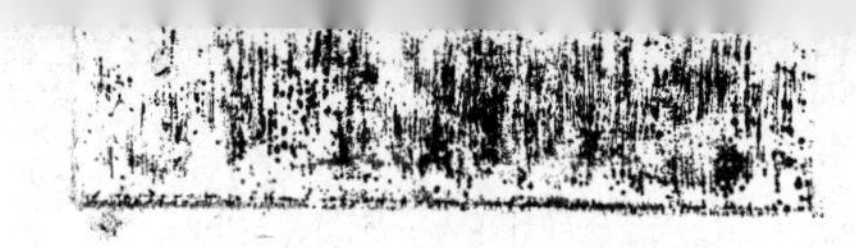